Population, Development and the Environment:
The Dynamic Interface

POPULATION, DEVELOPMENT AND THE ENVIRONMENT:
The Dynamic Interface

By

Dr. A.C.K. Nambiar
University of Calicut
Dr. John Matthai Centre
Aranattukara, Thrissur
Kerala

SERIALS PUBLICATIONS
New Delhi

First Published–2005

ISBN: 81-86771-59-X

Published by

Head Office

SERIALS PUBLICATIONS

4, B.S.S. Hall, Khyber Pass Market,
Civil Lines, Delhi–110054 (India)
Fax: 91-11-23812678
Phone: 23245225
e-mail: serials@satyam.net.in

Branch Office

4830/24, Prahlad Street, Ansari Road,
Darya Ganj, New Delhi-110002 (India)

Printed at :

Printed In India

Dedicated to my parents

Preface

Migration of people to resource rich areas in search of livelihood is as old as human history. This has acted as a powerful engine for the growth of world output in the post industrialization era. The movements now cut even the geographical boundaries of nations. India witnessed several migration currents over the centuries. Within India Kerala is the most migratory state. The state witnessed different patterns of migration and the one which sustained for decades and stood different from other migration currents was the migration of Travancore peasants to the Malabar region. Predominantly the migrants belonged to the poor strata of the Christian community. They were in search of their livelihood out of own farming. In the beginning thus there was only limited agenda in their mind. Fertile land was available in cheap then in Malabar. So they came to settle down permanently. Malabar was then underdeveloped and life especially in the highland regions where they settled was challenging and hazardous. With determination they withstood all the adversities. The migration in turn has brought about profound developmental impact on the economy of the region. In the process no doubt the migrants were able to improve their lot. This aroused in them more expectations and a bigger agenda developed in their mind and that was cultivation beyond subsistence level. Many were able to accomplish this. At the same time several side effects cropped up. They run on the lines of indiscriminate exploitation of the natural resource base of the region, deforestation, loss of wild life, widening inter community economic inequality, tribal land alienation, exploitation of the tribal etc. Here it is pertinent to note that if Kerala is "God's own country" Malabar can be said as the real "Abode of God" given the natural beauty of the region. This got defaced over the years due to this migration. I have been witnessing this development while traversing through some of these environmentally sensitive area of the region. This generated in me an interest to study the impact of migration. Fortunately the Indian Council of Social Science Research, New Delhi granted me a full time fellowship to study this issue. This enabled me to portray in this volume the various facets of developments witnessed by the Malabar region consequent upon the emergence of the settlements of Travancore peasants. The assistance provided by the Council is gratefully acknowledged.

In the course of the study in gathering information a number of individuals and institutions have extended unbound help in several ways. It is not possible to list all of them here. While placing on record my sincere thanks to all of them I will be failing in my duty if I do not thank in particular Mr. Biju Mathew who accompanied me in the course of the fieldwork.

Thanks are also due to M/s Serials Publications for publishing the manuscript neatly.

The development has not only by-passed certain sections of the society but also made their life much more miserable. To mention the plight of the scheduled tribes in pathetic. Their sufferings and disabilities are articulated in the book. So also certain policy suggestions to improve their lot is in order. I hope all this will generate some interest among the authorities to redeem the situation.

University of Calicut
Dr. John Matthai Centre
Aranattukara, Thrissur
Kerala

A.C.K. Nambiar

Contents

Chapter 1

Introduction

The process of economic development hinges largely upon the utilisation of available human and non human resources. The resources are however distributed unequally not only within the boundaries of a nation state but also between the nations. This necessitates the movement of factors within a nation to maximise the nation's output and also their movement across the nations to maximise the world output. No doubt material, capital and labour were mobile from the very inception of human civilization for more and better utilisation of available resources. By and large, the mobility was also unrestricted. In the modern age, though the dynamic changes in technology, particularly in transport and communication made it easier, faster and cheaper to navigate goods, capital, people and ideas than ever before with the emergence of the strong spirit of nation states restrictive policies to regularise the mobility of factors have come to be enforced to protect the domestic interests. Thus, mobility of factors became restricted. Of late, the globalisation policies are leading to a phenomenon in which there is an increasingly free flow of ideas, people, goods, services and capital. The direction of change is taking place in such a way as to make the national production system part of the global economy.

History of Human Migration

Though people moved from place to place in search of livelihood from the very inception of human civilization, migration in its modern form means the movement of people from labour surplus areas to areas of labour shortage began almost five centuries ago. It actually commenced with slavery. From the middle of the sixteenth century to the early nineteenth century more than 15 million people were taken from Africa to Europe, North America and Caribbean (Nayyar 1999:7). This was the largest enforced mass migration of labour in human history. With the abolition of slavery in the British Empire starting from 1830 for about fifty years there was exodus of people from India and China to work as indentured labour in mines, plantations and constructions in America, Caribbean's, South Africa, South East Asia and other distant lands. Though the destinations were mostly to the British, Dutch, French and German colonies the U S was another important destination where indentured labour also came from Japan. The exodus of people form Europe marked the next phase. This also occurred on a massive scale. Between 1870 and 1914 which may be considered as the first phase of globalisation it was estimated that more than 50 million people left Europe of whom two thirds went to Canada, Australia, New Zealand, South Africa, Argentina and Brazil (Nayyar 1999:7). This mass migration form Europe amounting to one eighth of its population in 1900 was mostly labour, displaced from the agricultural sector who could not find industrial employment. For some countries such as Britain, Italy,

Spain and Portugal such migration constituted as much as 20 to 40 percent of their population (Nayyar 1999:8).

The 1919-39 period was marked by subdued flow of workers. International migration almost came to an end with the First World War. Apart from war the restrictive migration laws and enforcement of passports on social and political reasons came to be practised. The Great Depression of 1930's further dampened the flow. At the same time, with the end of the Second World War there occurred massive movement of people within Europe. Most of them were refugees trying to settle. The late 1940's also witnessed emigration from Europe to the United States and Latin America. Coming to the second half of the 20th century two phases of international labour migration may be discerned.

In the first phase of migration which, started from late 1940's there were two distinct streams. While some moved from Europe to the United States, Canada, Australia and New Zealand driven by the search for economic opportunities others originating from the developing world, mostly Asia, North Africa and the Caribbeans moved to Western Europe. They were driven by the search for economic opportunities created out of economic growth combined with full employment.

During the second phase starting from the early 1970's migration to Europe almost came to a stop as immigration laws became much more restrictive every where. Thus to note, in 1967, Sweden established a stricter control on immigration and in March 1970 Switzerland adopted measures directed towards reducing the number of annual workers in its territory. By July 1971 France had taken steps to limit the number of Portuguese immigrants admitted annually and by November 1972 the Federal Republic of Germany assumed for the first time full responsibility for the recruitment of foreign workers. A turning point came in 1973-74. While in July 1973 Switzerland fixed a ceiling on the number of seasonal workers admitted annually, in November the Federal Republic of Germany stopped recruiting labour force from non-member states of the European Economic Community. In July 1974 France also followed suit. Thus most of the labour importing western countries tightened their immigration laws. In this phase also two different streams are discernable. Thus from the developing world to the United States there was a permanent immigration of people mostly persons with technical skills and professional qualifications, made possible by the change in immigration laws. In the second stream there was a temporary migration of people from labour surplus developing countries mostly unskilled/semi skilled workers into industrialised countries and to some of the developing countries where labour was scarce. The guest workers in Western Europe, the seasonal import of Mexican labour in the U S and the export of workers from South Asia, South East Asia and North Africa to the oil exporting countries of Middle East constituted this flow. The more recent import of temporary workers by labour scarce countries in East Asia is also one of the components of these temporary labour flows. Though the flow appears to be geographically somewhat diversified the major direction of flow seems to be toward the oil rich West Asian countries and rapidly industrialising East and South East Asian countries. A new trend in the flow has also emerged. Of late there is a consistent increasing trend in the international migration of women workers mainly as housemaids or entertainers. Such a trend emerged in response to two broad developments. Having housemaids to help the women of the households has become a matter of status and prestige for an increasing number of households in Middle East countries. In others there is increasing participation rate of females in gainful employment necessitating the employment of housemaids. On the whole what is significant is that international migration of people in search of work is laggard in the history. Some 2 to 3 million new migrants now leave developing countries in each year (both legally and illegally), about half of whom go to industrial countries. They send home about $ 75 billion a year about one third of the volume of net capital flows (World Bank 1995: 53)

While people moved beyond the nation's boundaries massive movement also occurred within the country. Thus sizable population distribution has taken place both within the developed and under developed countries. The movement consisted of rural to rural, rural to urban, urban to urban and urban to rural. The sizable drift of population was from rural to urban areas. For instance in USA of the total increase in the urban population of 24 million during the 1900-1920 period about nine million constituted migrants from farms and villages (Cherunilam 1987:64). During the 1920-30 decade, the U S Bureau of Agricultural Economics estimated the net loss in the farm population of USA due to migration at 6 million (Cherunilam 1987:64). In the 1940's and 50's this more or less doubled and became 11.4 million and 10. 1 million, respectively (Cherunilam 1987:64). Most of the shifts were to big cities. Since 1800 a net rural urban migration has taken place in all the European countries. The movement assumed importance at different times in various countries depending upon their stage of industrialisation and its magnitude. In this context it may also be noted that in most of the developed countries the contribution of rural urban migration to city growth is less significant when compared to the past. This is on account of the fact that urban growth has become unsustainable and farm population is approaching the minimum level. At the same time significant out-migration from cities is taking place in some of the countries. They move out from the core of cities to settle down in suburban fringes. As against this, urbanisation has gained more momentum in recent decades in the developing countries, mainly propelled by migration. In fact in some of the countries urban population is increasing beyond the absorptive capacity, resulting in over urbanisation. Between 1925 and 1950 at least 100 million people in the developing countries – about 10 percent of their rural population in 1925- migrated from the countryside to towns and cities. During the following 25 years the number rose to an estimated 330 million, equivalent to almost a quarter of the rural population of the developing countries (Cherunilam 1987:67). Bauroch estimated that between 1950 and 1970 migration from rural areas was responsible for 45 to 55 percent of the increase in urban population in the non-communist under developed countries (as quoted by Cherunilam 1987:66). What is important is that population movement within the rural and urban areas and temporary migration have undoubtedly involved even more people.

Globalisation and Migration

As globalisation has become the mantra for development, there is convergence in the economic policies of the nations. Questions have also been raised as to what is the impact of globalisation on the prospects of mobility of workforce and population movement? There is no doubt that workers around the world are living increasingly intertwined lives. However on the prospects of their mobility both optimistic and pessimistic notes are being made. One line of thinking is that capital can move to any country and commodities can be produced anywhere. Thus the emphasise seems to be on the need of production activities to move to areas where the labour and natural resources are unutilised or under utilised. Here the underlying assumption seems to be that it is far more difficult and costly to move labour to centres of production by making appropriate provision for them rather than shifting the production base. Thus it is argued that liberalisation may be associated with the growing immobility of workforce and population. During the past couple of decades when the constraints on the movement of commodities have been released or removed such constraints for the movement of people and labour in particular has been strengthened (Kundu and Shalini: 1996). At the same time it has also been advanced that globalisation is bound to exercise a significant influence in propelling the migration phenomenon. This is true of both internal and international migration. Some of the evidences are suggestive of this fact (Nayyar 1999). Accordingly it can be found that during the past twenty-five years there occurred divergence rather than convergence in levels of income between countries and people. In other words inequalities have increased during the last quarter of a century as the income gap between the rich and poor countries, between the rich and poor people within countries as also between the rich and poor in the world population has widened. There are also some other startling features in the development experiences of developing countries in the wake of economic liberalisation. Inequality in wages and income has registered an increase. Organized sector employment generation continues to lag behind the growth of labour force leading to the absorption of labour in an ever-increasing proportion in low productive casual and informal sectors. It is no surprise that the incidence of poverty has increased in most of the Latin American countries, Africa, the erstwhile Soviet block and some of the Asian countries. Thus push factors can be said to be as operative to increase emigration pressure. Side by side it has also been said that pull factors are operative in the industrialised countries. Firstly on the demand side technological possibilities for substitution of capital for labour are not unlimited in developed countries. Also while the possibilities of substituting trade flows for labour movements across national boundaries appear as large it may not be possible to do away with labour imports. For e.g. services are not tradable as goods. Also for agricultural sector there arises demand for labour, as unlike capital, land cannot be exported. So also once an economy reaches full employment it is exceedingly difficult if not impossible to reverse the initial flow of labour from the urban sector to the rural sector. Apart from all this it is also argued that globalisation may create conditions for the movement of labour across national boundaries. Thus while on the one side there are some attributes of globalisation which are conducive to and helpful for people who seek to cross borders in search of work and on the other side globalisation has set in motion forces which are creating demand for mobility across borders. Apart from all this it has also been advanced that globalisation itself may create conditions and unleash forces that could become an impetus for the movement of labour across national boundaries. The spread of electronic media and television the reach of which is quite extensive leads to global spread of cultural impulses. Thus, the alien culture and different languages are neither strange nor unexpected for the potential migrant whereby unification is taking place. Secondly revolution in transport and communication has slashed geographical barriers in terms of cost not only for the movement of goods, services, technology and finance but also for the movement of people. The introduction of internet with its array of web sites combined with the remarkable speed and the negligible cost of E-mail makes it much easier for the people to live away from their homes temporarily or even permanently. Thirdly globalisation in education taking place at a faster rate is unleashing fresh waves of population movements in various ways. The proportion of foreign students in the University system of major industrialised countries is increasing and many of them stay on. So also some of the labour exporting countries are increasingly adopting curricula that conform to international patterns and standards. Given the facilities of language such people are employable almost everywhere. Another source is the reach and spread of transnational corporations. In increasing number they recruit professionals globally for placements in its affiliates and adding to the movement of various categories of persons globally in various capacities. Altogether thus the chances of global movement of labour is poised for a further leap forward.

In this context it may also be argued that globalisation will promote internal migration. Regional disparities are fastly on the rise. Traditional sectors are in crisis leading to large-scale displacement of labour. Even in some of the modern sectors this is happening. All this will mean that labour has to move to places where opportunities are available.

Indian Migration

Though India was one of the most populated countries in the world, population movement in the Indian sub-continent was observed as relatively less in ancient times. The wide prevalence of the caste system, joint families, practice of early marriage, diversity of language and culture, lack of education and predominance of agriculture in the country were cited as some of the reasons for the immobility of the Indians (Davis: 1951). In spite of the above institutional rigidities, on a subdued scale there was migration. Thus before the emergence of migration in a big way from the first half of the 19th century on the introduction of indentured labour there was flow of people to various South East Asian countries. This was followed by the flow of workers by the turn of the 20th century mainly to Sri Lanka, Malaya and East African colonies. Besides labour the migrants consisted of businessmen, petty contractors, moneylenders, hawkers and educated professionals. The other pattern was mainly migration of educated persons and professionals from the twenties of the present century to United States of America and Europe.

In the wake of independence in 1947 the separation of India from Pakistan led to the relocation of over 15 million persons. But the net gain by India was estimated at about 70009. During the 1950's India gained about 1.2 to 1.3 million persons but the flow seems to have ebbed during the 1960's. Most of these migrants came from Assam and West Bengal what was then East Pakistan. Since the Bangladesh split from the rest of Pakistan in 1971 their influx to Assam has accelerated but no precise estimates are possible. This also coincided with the large-scale migration of labour to the Gulf region. Thus the emigration of Indians to Middle East as elsewhere during 1970's has partly set off this inflow into Eastern India. Thus international migration remained as an unimportant factor influencing population growth in the country (Visaria 1990:16).

Coming to internal migration a number of pull and push factors were in operation since the middle of the 19th century. The opening of plantations in Assam and in the Western Ghats, the starting of coal mining in Bihar, the growth of textile industry in Bombay and the construction of railways and other public works required large labour. On the other hand, there was in operation push factors like abject poverty, outbreak of famines, growing population, decline of rural industries and the feudal agrarian set up. Still voluntary movement occurred on a limited scale giving way for the shortage of labour in several of the provinces (Joseph 1988: 49). In the post independence period the accelerated development process gave impetus for the migration of people especially from rural to urban areas due to increasing industrialisation in urban areas. In 1971 the migration size was estimated at 661.75 lakh persons and by 1981 the size increased to 809.75 lakhs. Out of these 91.02 lakhs in 1971 and 108.10 lakhs in 1971 were inter state migration. In 1981 it was found that the dominant type of movement was rural to rural, 57.1 percent while it was 62 percent in 1971 followed by rural urban 16.5 percent in 1971 and 19.5 percent in 1981. Urban to urban migration was 13.6 percent in 1971 and 15.5 percent in 1981 and urban to rural 7.9 percent in 1971 and 7.9 percent in 1981 (Bhattacharya 1998: 1256). However one of the significant aspects to be noted is that the mobility of population in general has declined recently. This is the case with all types of migration. Interstate migration also declined perceptibly indicating that migrants are increasingly getting absorbed within their own states. This can possibly be due to social, economic and political factors.

Migration Scene in Kerala

Though the induction of indentured labour to the plantations resulted in the migration of some people from India in the first half of the 19th century indications were that migration from Kerala was very low. Migration from all the three erstwhile political units of Kerala started in a big way only from the third decade of the 20th century and the destination was Malaya, Burma, East Africa, Sri Lanka and Caribbean islands. For instance it is indicated that during the 1921-38 period there was an annual average out flow of 16529 persons from Kerala to Sri Lanka (Joseph 1988: 41). A set back to this flow came on account of the Great Depression and the Second World War. At the same time, the post war period witnessed new patterns of migration. Initially, there was the movement of more educated persons to USA and other continents. Kerala contributed no less significantly to this flow. The international migration from Kerala received the largest ever boost with the flow of workers to the Gulf countries. It is estimated that as many as 11.41 lakh Keralites now work in different parts of the world (3.6 percent of the population of the state) as per a study conducted by the

Dept. of Economics and Statistics of the Govt. of Kerala (as quoted in Hindu 2000). Some of the reports coming from Gulf countries indicate that Keralites constituted more than 50 percent of the total migrant labour in the region (Nair 1994: 105).

Coming to internal migration despite the demographic characteristics of an out- migrating region the erstwhile Travancore State was an in-migrating state till the Second World War. While a similar pattern prevailed in the Cochin State too the Malabar region was then a strong out-migrating region sending out streams of migrants in different directions including foreign lands (Joseph 1988). As against this with the outbreak of the Second World War the Travancore-Cochin region slowly transformed into an out-migrating region and it is estimated that the number of persons born in Travancore-Cochin but enumerated out side the State was 2.05 lakhs in 1951. Out of them 88275 were in Malabar (Census of India 1951: 5). The migration phenomenon gained further momentum in the State in the post independence period and the State emerged as one of the most migratory state in the country (Kamble 1983). There were several reasons to this. Though the performance of the state is outstanding in social development the economy is characterised by lop sided development leading to the problem of unemployment. Thus many migrated to other states as well as other countries.

Travancore Migration

In the history of migration Kerala witnessed a unique type of migration from the early decades of the last century and that was the migration of peasants. The flow originated from the Princely Travancore-Cochin

State and their main destination was Malabar, which formed part of the Madras Presidency. The flow started from the 1920's peaked in the 1930-50 period and though limited in size continued in the later decades too. In 1951 it was indicated that there were 88275 such migrants in Malabar (Census of India 1951:5). There were several distinct features to this migration. They were rural origin and predominantly belonged to the Christian community, especially Syrian Catholics. Thus some of the estimates shows that consequent upon this migration the Christian population in Malabar during the 1941-51 period showed a decennial percentage rise of 97.69 percent against 21.05 percent rise in the total population of Malabar during the decade (Tharakan 1978: 292). While some of them migrated individually others were in group with family and got settled permanently. It was in search of cultivable land. In Travancore, there was increased pressure on land due to increase in population and commercialisation of agriculture with the introduction of plantations. At the same time, the availability of vast areas of underdeveloped land, conducive climate and soil conditions in Malabar acted as pull factors. Naturally peasants started to move out of Travancore and their main destination was Malabar. Their settlements were in uninhabited hilly tracts.

Objectives of the Study

As migration takes place in a large societal framework it has wider impacts. This is particularly the case with the peasant migrants of Travancore. Most importantly what is the outcome of this specific migration at the household level as far as the migrant and his family are concerned? Was their mission successful and did it lead to the betterment of the economic conditions? What were their sufferings and did the migrant and his family get integrated with the society? These are the crucial questions that need to be probed. No systematic attempt has so far been made to examine these issues. In the case of these migrants the problems they encountered in the beginning were formidable and sufferings untold (due to attack of malaria, threat to life and crops from wild animals etc.). Also as migrants of this type belong to the poor strata and as economic status and education are factors in absorption the problem of integration becomes much more painful.

Migration of this type can also bring profound developmental impact not only in the economy of the region but also in the social, political and cultural life of the people of the region. Introduction of new crops, cultivation practices, development of markets, industrialisation, infrastructure developments, social structure, change in cultural practices and institutions, etc. is one dimension of this process. Introduction of new value systems of thrift, work culture, living pattern etc could be another. In the field of education and health development too their contribution can be hypothesised as significant as in the social sector development in the state the role of the Christian community and church was observed as strong. They can also be expected to have spearheaded in mobilising to fight for social causes and in introducing new dimensions to the political structure of the region. With the emergence of a more plural society it can also be said that there is visible change in the societal value systems, culture and social institutions- a move towards socialisation. Altogether it can be hypothesised that dynamic changes have been brought about in the region on the economic, political and social front consequent upon migration.

The social conflicts and other social costs of migration too can be said as significant in the particular case. Land records as reported in the region were most unsatisfactory and land transactions one of oral. The scope for encroachment thus kept wide open will mean much conflict at individual and group level. A plural society can have its own social problems. Tales of these conflicts and sufferings were unheard outside. Much more serious is the problem of deforestation consequent upon migration. There was indiscriminate encroachment on forestland. Here the interest of scheduled tribes too has come into conflict and the dimensions of all this needs to be explored. Also the introduction of new crops and cultivation practices will have its adverse effect on the environment.

In the light of all this the overall objectives of the study will be to examine;

(a) The impact of migration on the economy of the region and the environment

(b) The socio-economic conditions of the migrant and non migrant households and

(c) The impact of migration on the social and economic life of the native population.

Methodology

The study is with reference to the Pulpally village situated in the Sultan Battery taluk of Wayanad district. There were special reasons for the selection of the village. While migration brought about total transformation of the village economy there was also epoch making events on the social and political fronts. The village had also population inhabitation for centuries and this consisted of tribal and non-tribal population. Even some of the events in Ramayana are said to have occurred in the village. For detailed study four hundred households were randomly selected from the village. For the selection of the households the following methodology was adopted. Within the village there were areas (Panchayat wards) where the originals and migrants were somewhat concentrated. Thus 2 wards having large concentration of migrants and 2 wards having large concentration of native households were identified from the Panchayat on discussion with the ward level representatives and by looking into the Panchayat registers. A list of households of the wards was separately prepared as migrants and natives based on the Panchayat register and on discussion with the ward members. From the list of migrant households 200 households and from the list of native households 100 Non-Tribal and 100 Tribal households were drawn by random sample method for detailed study. A questionnaire was prepared and by personal interview method the data was collected from the sample households in 1999. Also the investigation stretched to detailed discussion with the native households, the migrants, the official functionaries in the village, social and political activists etc to develop a perspective about pre-migration village economy, the people and their life and the consequences of migration. Thus both qualitative and quantitative data was collected. There was overwhelming response from the sample households and other respondents as the local level ward members and some of the prominent local individuals helped in getting us introduced to a number of households. Inspite of this it was found that the data of some of the households were of doubtful validity and hence they were eliminated from the final analysis. Thus for the final analysis there was 381 households comprised of 194 migrant households and 187 non-migrant households (96 Non-Tribal households called Chetties and 91 Tribal households).

To study the impact of migration the pre-migration socio-economic structure and living conditions of the people was depicted. In this background the current social and economic structure of the village, the people and their social and economic status was examined. The economic structure of the village was examined in terms of the economic activity and the availability of social and economic infrastructure. The social and economic status of the households were examined in terms of education, housing conditions, occupational structure, land and other assets ownership, consumption expenditure, indebtedness etc. The differential performance of households was highlighted by analysing these aspects by migrant and non-migrant households. A special note is made on the status of the Tribes, the overall impact of migration on them and on the environment.

Plan of the Study

The study is presented in eight chapters. The first chapter gives the introduction, objectives and the methodology of the study. This is followed by a brief review of literature. In the third chapter a brief account about the study area, its population and their early economic and social life is given. The migration process, about the migrants and their initial living problems are outlined in the fourth chapter. The impact of migration on the economic and social structure is discussed in the fifth chapter. An examination of the socio-economic status of the population forms the subject matter of the sixth chapter. The seventh chapter deals with the ill effects of migration, the problems and prospects of the area. The eighth chapter provides an overall summary of the findings and some of the recommendations.

REFERENCES

Bhattacharya Prabir (1988), The Informal Sector and Rural to Urban Migration: Some Indian Evidence, Economic and Political Weekly, May 23.

Census of India (1951), Travancore Cochin Part I, Subsidiary Tables, Emigration.

Cherunilam Francis (1987), Migration, Causes, Correlates, Trends and Policies, Himalaya Publishing House, Bombay.

Davis K (1951), Population of India and Pakistan, Priceton University Press, New Jersey.

Hindu- A National Daily in English (2000), July 22.

Joseph K V (1988), Migration and Economic Development of Kerala, Mittal Publications, Delhi.

Kamble N D (1983), Labour Migration in Indian States, Ashish Publishing House, New Delhi.

Kundu A and Shalini Gupta (1996), Migration, Urbanisation and Regional Inequality, Economic and Political Weekly, Dec. 28.

Nair Gopinathan P R (1994), Migration of Keralites to the Arab World in Prakash B A (ed.) Kerala's Economy- Performance, Problems and Prospects, Sage Publications, New Delhi.

Nayyar Deepak (1999), Globalisation and Migration: Retrospect and Prospect, Labour and Development, Vol. 4 No 1&2, June.

Tharakan Michael (1978), Dimensions and Characteristics of the Migration of Farmers from Travancore to Malabar 1930-1950, Journal of Kerala Studies, June.

Visaria Pravin (1990), Population Growth and Development in India- A Perspective for the 8th Plan, Yojana, Jan 26.

World Bank (1995), World Development Report, Washington.

Chapter 2

Migration–A Review of Theoretical and Empirical Studies

Migration is a worldwide phenomenon. This is true of all types of migration such as international, internal, urban and rural. What distinguishes one from the other is the size of migration, its causes and consequences. This calls for migration specific studies. No doubt various facets of some of the migration streams were subjected to intense study and debate. Thus on various issues related to migration theoretical propositions were made and they were subject to further empirical testing. This chapter makes an attempt to review some of these studies in the light of the theory of migration. First let us consider some of the theoretical underpinnings.

Though sustained migration occurred in the post industrial revolution era systematic attempts to understand the process started only later. The origin was a little more than a century ago. Ravenstein made the pioneering attempt. Based on an analysis of the 1881 British Census and subsequently drawing data from more than 20 countries he came to observe that movements largely occurred from area of low opportunity to area of large opportunity and migration gets accelerated with the growth of transport, communication, trade and industry. Migration also occurred in steps that the movement was from rural to nearby towns and then to large cities. While most of the migrants moved to short distance the long distance migrants moved to large centres of commerce. Families dominated among the short distance migrants (Ravenstein 1885). According to him migration currents were also produced as a result of bad or oppressive laws, social surroundings, heavy taxation, unattractive climate, uncongenial surroundings and even compulsion. Though many of his findings have been empirically proved as sound some of the observations were not found as applicable in the case of certain migration currents. For instance the observation that families predominate among short distance migrants appears to be not valid in many parts of Africa and Asia. Studies have also found that there is not enough evidence to support Ravenstein's generalisation that migration proceeds step by step (U N 1973). Being a post industrial revolution phenomenon migration has essentially been viewed as linked to urban industrial growth. One of the earliest proponents of this view was Lewis who emphasised the contributions of labour mobility to capital formation in the cities (Lewis W A 1954). Ranis and Fei later developed the theory in a dual economy framework where there is the subsistence agricultural sector and modern industrial sector (Ranis and Fee 1961). The agricultural sector in an underdeveloped economy is characterised by the existence of surplus labour and zero marginal productivity. Such labour is available at a subsistence wage and the urban industrial sector is able to draw labour from the rural sector, without incurring any loss to the rural sector. The model is also an endorsement of the Marxian analysis of the working of the capitalist economy. Accordingly the urban sector is characterised by dynamism. Capital accumulation facilitated by the reinvestment of surplus and technical change increases the share of profits to rise in the national income. This further leads to the accumulation of capital. As urban wages are at a premium (say 30 percent) there is sufficient inducement for labour to shift. The wage is assumed as constant and supply of labour as elastic. The wage gap between the rural and urban area is explained in several ways. Part of the difference can be said as illusory as there is high cost of living in the capitalist sector. Substantial difference however exist on account of the psychological cost of transferring from the easy going way of life of the subsistence sector to the more regimented or urbanised environment of the capitalist sector. The difference is also advanced as recognition of the fact that even the unskilled worker is of more use to the capitalist sector having been there for some time than the new recruits. Also it has to be noted that there is difference in standards that workers in the capitalist sector acquires. Thus the difference in tastes and social prestige has to be recognised and provided for by way of the offer of higher wages by the urban capitalist sector. The employment expansion is assumed to continue until all surplus labour is absorbed in the urban industrial sector. Thereafter the labour supply curve becomes positively slopped and both urban wages and employment will continue to grow. Thus structural transformation of the economy takes place and the process of industrial modernisation will increasingly dominate the overall economy. Though the model is in conformity with the historical experiences of economic growth in the West some of the tenets of the model such as the rate of labour absorption in the modern sector, the availability of surplus labour in the agricultural sector, full employment in the modern sector and the assumption of constancy of urban real wages until the absorption of surplus labour are open to doubt. It is said that with capital accumulation and higher growth technical dynamism leads to low rate of labour absorption and the tendency of the wages is to rise substantially.

Sjaastad developed the model of human investment theory (See Sasikumar 1999). It is argued that there is a cost and benefit analysis behind migration decisions and people will migrate when the benefit outweighs costs. Difference in income between the origin and place of destination constitutes the benefits. This has to be discounted and the present value arrived at. Costs include moving expenses, opportunity costs of foregone earnings between jobs and non-monetary psychic costs such as disutility of leaving one's home community. It has been propounded that the educated youth tend to be more mobile because the lifetime income difference between the area of origin and destination is large. So also psychic costs of educated are less, as they are more adaptive.

According to Todaro migration proceeds in response to rural urban difference in expected income rather than actual earnings (Todaro 1969). The process will continue until the expected urban income is equal to the expected rural income. Todaro's basic model and its extension consider the urban labour force distributed between relatively small modern sector and a large traditional sector. Most of them are engaged in the traditional sector where wage level is low. The basic behavioural assumption of the model is that migrants consider the various labour market opportunities available to them and choose the one that maximise the expected gain. There is the risk of getting an urban job as vast unemployment prevails even in the urban areas. The expected gain is therefore a function of :1) the existing rural urban real wage differential that prevails for different skills and educational categories of workers and 2) the degree of probability of new migrant obtaining an urban job. Thus migration is primarily stimulated by rational economic considerations of relative benefits and costs, financial as well as psychological. The decisions to migrate depend on expected rather than actual wage differential where the expected differential is determined by the interaction of two variables stated above. The probability of obtaining an urban job is inversely related to the urban unemployment rate. Migration rates in excess of growth in urban job opportunities are not only possible but also rational and even likely in the face of wide urban rural expected income differentials. High rates of urban unemployment are therefore an inevitable outcome of the serious imbalance in economic opportunities between urban and rural areas of less developed countries. The rural urban migration seen as an outcome of rational decisions based on the application of the theory of probability is less realistic as migration takes place on ignorance about the unemployment situation in the urban areas. Also the model takes into account only economic factors though non-economic factors too influence the decision to migrate.

According to Lee, the decision to migrate and the process of migration are influenced by four important factors such as: 1) factors associated with the area of origin 2) factors associated with the area of destination 3) intervening factors and 4) personal factors (Lee 1966).

In every area there is usually two or three set of factors that influence the decision to migrate. While one set of factors attracts people to it the other set of factors tend to repel people from the area. There may also be another set of factors to which people are usually indifferent. Migration is influenced by these sets of factors in combination with the intervening obstacles and personal factors. Besides the factors associated with the origin and destination and the intervening obstacles there are many personal factors that facilitate or retard migration. Accordingly personal sensitiveness, intelligence and awareness of conditions elsewhere influence the migration decision. At the same time the knowledge of the situation at the destination depends upon personal contacts or upon source of information, which are not universally available. In addition to personal characteristics like attitude towards change, adventurism, enterprise, emotional factors, ambition etc. also affect the decision to migrate. It may also be mentioned that in the case of a large number of people the migration is associational migration like wife migrating with the husband or children migrating with parents.

On the migration phenomenon the neo classical approach has been challenged in recent years. A key insight into this approach reveals the fact that migration decisions are not made by isolated individual actors, but by larger units of related people- typically families or households. According to this approach people act collectively not only to maximise expected income, but also to minimise risks and to loosen constraints associated with a variety of market failures apart from those in the labour market (Katz and Stark 1986, Stark 1991, Stark and Levhari 1982). Stark has incorporated into this model two additional explanatory variables – desire for leisure and aversion to work. The model notes that the motive is not expected income maximisation as such. Maximisation of familial leisure and familial aversion to risk is another (Stark 1983). While Mincer explored the effect of husband-wife family ties on the probability of migration (Mincer 1978) Borjas considered the welfare of children as a critical explanatory variable in the migration decision (Borjas 1990). To develop a model of migration Tcha used urban to rural income ratio (the rate of the weighted average of blue collar and white-collar income in urban areas to farm income). He found this income ratio as more effective than the income ratio traditionally used to explain the aggregate migration (Tcha 1996). The absence of well-developed banking and credit accessibility to poor, the absence of institutional mechanism to invest and diversify income too leads to migration. It has also been argued that the search for new income sources promotes migration even if income does not necessarily increase. They also argue that workers migrate not only to improve income in absolute terms but also to increase income relative to other households and hence to reduce their relative deprivation compared to some reference groups (Stark 1991). Thus it has been postulated that it is family or household units, which are the appropriate units of analysis of migration research. Wage differential is not a necessary condition as incentive to diversify risk is a factor. Given the situation the governments can influence the migration rates not only through policies that influence labour markets but also policies that develop insurance markets and capital markets.

There are also further dimensions to the cause of migration. It can be traced to the land reform measures in specific cases. According to Connel the break up of large holdings in Iran decreased the demand for hired labour, which is not fully offset in the new small farms, which are predominantly family operated. This led to unemployment and migration of labour. Also collectivist reforms has led to such ill effects especially when land managers are induced to adopt labour replacing innovations leading to the displacement of labour. Thus it was noted that some of the migration to Santiago and Valpariso was by landless thus replaced (Connel John 1976). According to the observation of the UN the migration from the countryside to cities bears a close functional relation to the process of industrialisation, technological advancement and other cultural changes, which characterise the evolution of modern society in almost all parts of the world (UN 1953). It has been found that the main factors determining the rate of outward movement is the expansion of employment in other occupations. It is this factor, which explains the high rate of movement in the 1960's in some of the advanced countries and in rapidly developing countries in Latin America, Middle East and Africa according to a study of International Labour Organisation (cited by Savani 1996). In a sense there is policy bias which creates a strong incentive to expand economic activities in the urban than rural areas encouraging people to move to urban areas in the expectation of better job opportunities and better access to services (World Bank 1978). As to the reason for migration demographic features are also at work. According to the U N observation high rural fertility with reduction in mortality rate lead to high rural population and migration to urban areas (U N 1953).

Globalisation policies have been adopted by most of the countries. What impact does it make on international migration? Nayyar examined the various facets of this aspect. Examining the pros and cons of globalisation on the labour market behaviour he comes to the conclusion that market driven conditions and institutions created by globalisation will sustain perhaps even increase cross border flows. He has dealt with the various factors that influence the supply and demand factors (Nayyar 1999). Here it is important to point out the dimensions of international migration. Russel and Teitelbaum estimate that in 1989 official migrants remittance amounted to more than the total official development assistance to developing countries in the year. It also represented the second largest trade flow after oil sales (Russel and Teitelbaum 1992).

As to the factors that encourage migration a number of empirical observations have been made in the country. Observations are somewhat complex and dynamic changes have taken place over the years in the pattern of migration. Studying the 1961 migration pattern in India Kundu and Gupta conclude that the spatial disparity in development among other things led to migration. Thus the backward states had higher rates of migration while the developed states were absorbing these migrants. However recent experiences showed that though regional disparity has widened, size of migration has gone down. Thus the developed states in 1990's reports a much lower percentage of in-migration than the previous decades. As a corollary to this out-migration from the backward states have also gone down (Kundu and Gupta 1996). Explanations to this has been offered by some researchers in terms of growing assertion of regional identity, education (up to high school) in regional language, adoption of master plans and land use restrictions at the city level etc. as all these directly or indirectly discourage migration. This seriously discounts the proposition that the mobility of the factors of production operationalised through the market would automatically ensure optimal distribution of economic activities in space (Kundu 1986). Also complementary explanations are provided in terms of increase in inter state inequality in the post independence period. In each state a few large cities – usually the state capitals-emerged as centres of industrial investment as they have an advantage of having an industrial base and large level of basic services. These centres received a large chunk of subsidised amenities provided through their State governments and attracted elites, professionals and industrialists. At the same time most of the backward regions or districts got neglected and this resulted in the movement of people from backward to developed regions within the State. Also it was noted that growth of agriculture was extremely uneven in space due to the strategy adopted in the 1950's and early 1960's. This sharpened the inequalities and encouraged intra-state migration particularly from rural to urban areas. Further, with the decline of inter-state migration the small and medium sized towns located in the backward states are absorbing migrants from the hinderlands (Kundu and Gupta 1996). Scholars have also advanced further explanations in terms of the development programmes initiated by the states. This has led to a situation in which need for mobility is felt less as people are now able to earn for their living at their own place. The development of education, health, communication and transport facilities too have come to influence this trend (Merhotra G K 1974).

On the migration pattern Alagh and others have advanced the operation of a suction mechanism within the Indian agrarian system. Accordingly regions with high and growing land productivity are able to attract migrant labourers from other regions. This, they believe, results in the equalisation of labour productivity in space (Alagh et al. 1978). Moorthy attempted to examine the rural to rural migration as it has gained significance. It was found that distant migration takes place even in the absence of inter-state wage differentials or growth differentials. Minimum statutory wages have a negative influence on rural to rural in-migration. Where as the growth rate of S D P originating from agriculture do not have any significant influence on the level of migration (Moorthy et.al 1999). Based on the sample survey data analysis of selected cities in India Acharya comes to the conclusion that adverse economic condition is the most important single cause of migration to cities (Acharya G N 1964).

On the reason for migration a study in Orissa revealed that the motivating factor is search for livelihood as most of the migrants belonged to the land less and marginal landholders. However they were faced with several problems of unhygienic and hazardous working conditions, poor living conditions and hence were victims of health problems. At the same time as wages received were high they were able to remit regularly and make improvement in the living conditions of family. At the same time it was also noted that migration caused family disintegration, degradation of morality and value systems and lack of human touch (Thripathy and Dash 1997).

Attempts have also been made to relate migration and political background of the emigrating regions. Rao finds that more than a third of the respondents in Bhilai town moved from Andhra Pradesh, Kerala and West

Bengal where communism was very popular. So also it has been found that large scale out migration occurred from states where regional parties were influential (Rao 1977). Similarly in his study of migrants in Pune Nair observed that a number of them left Tamil Nadu because of lack of job opportunities. Job opportunities to certain communities were less due to the anti Brahmin policy followed by the Dravida Munneta Kazhakom government (Nair 1978).

Based on a survey and resurvey of six villages within the district of Satara Kumudini and Bhate noted out migration and in-migration in the villages as higher than expected. Female movement occurred due to marriage and this balanced the male outward movement only to some extent. This hints at the economic incapability of the male to take his wife with him when he moved to urban areas. With a lag of 9 years they were able to take them. The balancing of female movement with the male seemed healthier when the males moved into the villages (Kumudini and Bhate 1975).

Another study covering 400 villages spread over 7 states notes that majority of the migrants were adult male, married and on balance educationally more advanced than their fellow villagers. Overwhelming majority of working migrants came from self-employed agricultural and non-agricultural households. The analysis of the village characteristics associated with migration showed that land shortage, low fertility of land and squeezed distribution of land induced people to migrate (Dasgupta and Laishley 1975).

Urbanisation, industrialisation and migration are closely interlinked. Industrialisation leads to migration from rural to urban areas as a response to urban industrial development. So also migration is considered as a major factor of urbanisation and industrialisation. Here migrants are considered dynamic agents of urbanisation process. Dupont examined the latter case with reference to Jetpur. The study notes that migration has played a major role in the expansion of the urban economy by increasing the labour supply as well as the labour force participation rate of the urban population. There were also in-migrant entrepreneurs who contributed substantially to industrial development in terms of qualified human resources and transfer of capital. An upward social mobility was noticed and migration was a pre requisite to benefit from this process (Dupont 1992).

The informal sector has been one of the powerful sectors for urban growth. Bhattacharya examined the role of informal sector in the rural urban migration making use of the Census data. It was found that far from being a passive absorber of labour the informal sector is dynamic and productive in attracting and sustaining labour on its own rights. Paradoxically even when the formal sector growth had grown at a lower rate the relative contribution of migration to urban growth was increasing during the 1970's. Clearly this occurred on account of the important role played by the informal sector (Bhattacharya 1998).

Migration associated social problems are many. However a communal perspective in respect of the conflict has not been attempted and Banu's attempt run on this line with respect to Surat riots. It has been found that the migrants in Surat are attempting to emphasize their ethnic identification and access to power by struggle. This is leading to communal riots. Thus migration intensifies and strengthens the ethnicities and class-consciousness. All this ultimately results in violence (Banu 1994). More or less on similar lines run the findings of Engineer (Engineer 1994). He too noted that there is widespread feeling of insecurity on the part of the migrants, which brutally exploits them. They have nothing but contempt. The riot was in response to their anger and frustration.

In-migration by land hungry peasants in India has led to a major change in the demographic composition in several regions in India. Assam is one of the States, which has witnessed profound migration during the first decade of the 20th century alienating the Tribes from the land. Not to speak of Tribes even the Muslims were alienated and driven out of their land. It has been found that apart from land alienation and loss of identity, tribes felt an acute sense of insecurity in their mind. Even most of the development was concentrated in the non-Tribal areas, which further deepened their wounds. All this got culminated in the emergence of Tribal organisations. They are demanding political power and social justice by organising riots in which the native population cutting across communities have participated (Misra 1999).

A significant development in the agriculturally prosperous regions like Punjab and Haryana is the growth of capitalist agriculture. It was sustained by the migrant labour and the plight of labour was a matter of serious concern. Studies have found that the migrant labour is employed in gross violation of all the labour welfare measures including Minimum Wages Act and that their working conditions were equivalent to that of slaves. Helpfully there is organised labour trade and emergence of recruiting agents in most of the agriculturally prosperous areas (Singh 1997).

The impact of migration has been an intensely debated subject. The impact is all round and complex in nature. Examining the issues Taylor and Adelman note with reference to the Mexican village that a near self-sufficient economy has got integrated with the national and consumer market on migration. While large remittance, consequent upon international migration, generated first round growth effects on village income, consumption and investment it has generated important second and higher rounds remittance effect. This second and higher order remittance effect was rarely considered in remittance use studies (Taylor Edward J and Adelman Irma 1996). It was also noted that international migration opportunities are household specific, say due to international network of elites and this could further accentuate adverse distributional effects by preventing the spread of information (Rodriguez 1998). At the same time in Philippines the author notes that as labour exports have received active support from government and in general emigration has improved social welfare. Here observations of other studies are worth mentioning. It has been found that international remittances reduced inequality in one village in Mexico but increased in another (Stark et.al 1986). At the same time using the longitudinal data for the two Mexican villages Taylor observed that the unequalising effect on household income distribution declined over time (Taylor 1992). Adams on the other hand reports that inequality was on the increase in Egypt and Rural Pakistan because of international emigration (Adams 1989,

Adams 1992). In rural India Upreti noted remittance as one of the consequences of migration (Upreti 1992). There exists a negative relation between income and remittance. The other significant impact were that they carried urban ideas, customs, practices, the urban work discipline, the concept of job with a fair wage, ideas of health and hygiene, usefulness of education, medicine etc.

In underdeveloped countries urbanisation has taken place at a faster rate and urban social and economic problems have become endemic. This has led to the phenomenon of push back according to Ashish. Thus, urban areas faced with high unemployment rates and also high under employment act as deterrents to the flow of migrants on a fresh basis. Even if employment opportunities exist in urban areas the first person to get absorbed is the marginally employed already residing in the urban areas unless of course special skills are required. Thus paradoxically rapid urban population growth becomes a factor in slowing down the rate of migration from rural to urban areas. This is quite contrary to the push theory they would make us to believe (Ashish 1978).

Remittance associated with migration has been cited as a key benefit out of migration, not only by replacing foregone income, but augmenting savings, investment and technological innovation. In the context of inter urban and rural urban migration, an attempt was made to throw light on the spread effects particularly through remittance by Jayasri. The study found that there is substantial linkage effect from the towns leading to the growth of hinterlands of West Bengal. At the same time there are variations in the degree of spread effect in different regions in India (Jayasri 1993).

Kerala has been identified as one of the most migratory states in India. This is true of families also. It was also rural to rural followed by rural urban migration. In the state high population pressure, low per capita income and lack of employment opportunities forced many people to migrate to other states. To a large extent it has also been noted that the people of the state are dynamic and more mobile compared to the population of other states. Further the social and cultural background of the population is said as motivating them to migrate. Another distinguishing feature observed is that the Kerala out migrants do not return to their native place even on retirement/old age compared to other migrants (Kamble 1983).

A very significant development on the migration front in Kerala is the Gulf bound migration. Attempts have also been made to unravel the various dimensions of this migration. It was found that the Gulf migrants are less educated and are mostly engaged in menial jobs though a limited number were educated and professionals. The remittance has contributed substantially to the household prosperity of the migrants. However the developmental impact of the migration was found as limited since most of the remittance was used for conspicuous consumption (Nair 1987, Nambiar 1995).

Coming specifically to the migration of the Travancore people to Malabar attempts have been made to examine the various facets of this migration. The earliest attempt to examine the history, the causes and consequences of this migration was attempted by

Tharakan (Tharakan 1978). In accordance with his observation the flow started from 1920's and continued in the later decades too on a significant scale. Based on a review of the population statistics of the region it was found that by 1951 there were about 70000 Travancore migrants in Malabar. It was the rapidly increasing population and consequent pressure on land in Travancore in the early decades of the present century that pushed farmers from Travancore to Malabar. Commercialisation of agriculture and the development of plantations in Travancore in this period too aided this process. As to the features of the migrants it has been noted that they were mainly Christians belonging to the Syrian Catholic rite. The impact of the flow was mainly felt in rural tracts of Malabar particularly the taluks of Wayanad, Kozhikod, Kottayam and Kurumbanad. The study also notes that there occurred significant decline in the forest area in the region as a result of this migration. The hardships the early migrants suffered on various accounts such as attack of wild animals, diseases, lack of basic facilities etc. also found reference in the study. Joseph attempted to look into this migration in a historical perspective making use of the secondary sources of information (Joseph 1988). This was supplemented by a very brief sample survey of migrants in selected settlements. After examining the socio-economic structure of the Travancore region he comes to the conclusion that there was an escalation of the levels of aspirations and diversification of wants in general in the area. One of the contributing factors for this development was education related awakening, infusion of progressive ideas and the accompanying desire for material improvement. Also high export prices of hill products led to an unsatisfied demand for land in the area and in this situation people were on the move in search of more land. Migration and their settlement in Malabar were mainly financed out of land sale as land sale proceeds accounted for 85 percent of the capital with which they came. Catholics were the largest group of migrants. They were marginal farmers. He also observed that the families, which migrated, were mostly the descendants of earlier immigrants in the region. The study also takes stock of the social problems faced by the migrants in the new settlements. The locals looked them down, they were socially segregated and there was social tension. But open clashes were not observed. The Church provided inspiring leadership and as stated the priests acted as friend, philosopher and guide then to the migrants. The migrants also showed unity in the midst of hostility of the natives. The study noted that migration has been instrumental for the development of the Malabar district. Also apart from significant capital formation, change in cropping pattern to cash crops there was spread effects on the locals as well as in the region. Migration also led to the large economic betterment of the migrants. At the same time the study recognises that migration has its cost too and it was deforestation. This migration has made deep impact on the economic and social life of the tribal population in Malabar. This aspect was examined by Mohandas (Mohandas 1992). The study also notes that the migrants were from the Southern districts of Kerala especially Kottayam and Idukki. The main motivation was cultivation in government and puramboku land including forests. Tribal land alienation was one of the serious social consequences of migration. On this the study notes that one third of the households covered by the study had lost part of their land especially to the settlers. At the sample level the average area held prior to the immigration was 267 cents of which 124 cents,

46.44 percent were reported to be thus alienated. It occurred in a variety of ways such as mortgages ultimately leading to the take over, fictitious claims, encroachment and in few cases outright sale. By and large the simple, straightforward and innocent character of the Tribes are said as exploited by some of the settlers to grab the land. As to the restoration the study notes that most of the tribes did not possess valid titles to property to establish the right of possession. Lack of adequate administrative set up, problem in the valuation of costs incurred in developing the land and organised opposition from settlers has also rendered the efforts at restoration impractical. The land has also been transferred several times making it further difficult to administer the restoration of the land to the tribes. The study also notes that the tribes are in acute poverty as 52.20 percent of the households were below the poverty line. Even in the case of the infrastructure which is developed the tribes benefited peripherally and it was a trickling down effect. Also lack of assets and bad housing conditions were some of the other important observations of the study. Besides alcoholism it has been noted that the migrants are prone to several kinds of illegal activities at the influence of the migrants and they run on the line of illegal felling of trees, transportation of illegal items like narcotics, sandalwood, ivory collection etc. The migration has also impacted upon them in several forms. Economic deprivation caused by the destruction of traditional life support system, casualisation, reduction in self-employment, dependency on the market system through monetisation of all transactions and addiction to liquor are some of them. At the same time the settlers created demonstration effect with respect to cropping pattern, adoption of new technology and self-employment programmes like dairy. On the social front the role of Mooppan has declined and the social evils like dowry is on the rise.

From a brief review of migration studies attempted above it can be seen that as far as the causes and consequences of migration is concerned there are diverging observations. Some of the features are also specific to certain migration currents and this calls for migration specific studies. Though isolated attempts have been made to examine the various facets of Travancore migration a systematic and comprehensive attempt leaves much to be desired. In this context the study assumes significance.

REFERENCES

Acharya, G.N. (1964), Some Thoughts on Urbanisation, Yojana, Sept.13.

Adams, Richard (1989), Worker Remittances and Inequality in Rural Egypt, Economic Development and Cultural Change, (38).

Adams, Richard (1992), The Effects of Migration and Remittances on Inequality in Rural Pakistan, Pakistan Development Review, 931.

Alagh Y.K., Bhaduri A and Bhalla G.S. (1978), Labour Absorption in Indian Agriculture- Some Explanatory Investigation in Agriculture Growth and Manpower Absorption in India, I L O, Geneva.

Banu Zainab (1994), Immigrant Groups as a Factor in Communal Riots, Economic and Political Weekly, Sept. 10.

Bhattacharya Prabir (1998), The Informal Sector and Rural to Urban Migration-Some Indian Evidence, Economic and Political Weekly, May 23.

Borjas, G. (1990), Intergenerational Mobility of Immigrants, Dept. of Economics, University of Chicago (Mimeographed).

Bose Ashish (1978), India's Urbanisation 1901-1971, Tata Mc Graw Hill Publishing Co, New Delhi.

Cornwell John, et.al. (1976), Migration from Rural Areas, Oxford University Press, Delhi.

Dasgupta Biplab and Laishley Roy (1975), Migration from Villages, Economic and Political Weekly, Oct.18.

Dupont Veronique (1992), Impact of In-migration on Industrial Development-Case Study of Jetpur in Gujrat, Economic and Political Weekly, Nov.7.

Engineer Irfan (1994), Backward Communities and Migrant Workers in Surat Riot, Economic and Political Weekly, May 28.

Jayasri Ray Chaudhari (1993), Migration and Remittances-Inter Urban and Rural Urban Linkages, Sage Publications, New Delhi.

Joseph K V (1988), Migration and Economic Development of Kerala, Mittal Publications, Delhi.

Kamble M D (1983), Labour Migration in Indian States, Ashish Publishing House, New Delhi.

Katz and Stark (1986), Labour Migration and Risk Aversion in Less Developed Countries, Economic Development and Cultural Change, Vol 31.

Kumudini Dandekar and Vaijayanti Bhate (1975), Socio-economic Change During the Three Five Year Plans (Based on a Study of Rural Communities During 1953-66), Arthavijnana, No.4, Dec.

Kundu (1986), Migration, Urbanisaiton and Inter-regional Inequality, Economic and Political Weekly, Nov. 15.

Kundu Amitabh and Shalini Gupta (1996), Migration, Urbanisation and Regional Inequality, Economic and Political Weekly, Dec. 28.

Lee E S (1966), A Theory of Migration, Demography, Vol.3.

Lews W Arthur (1954), Economic Development with Unlimited Supply of Labour, Manchester School of Economics and Social Studies, Vol 22.

Merhrotra, G. K. (1974), Birthplace Migration in India, Census of India, 1971, Special Monograph No.1, Govt. of India, New Delhi.

Mincer J. (1978), Family Migration Decisions, Journal of Political Economy, (86).

Misra Udayon (1999), Immigration and Identity Transformation in Assam, Economic and Political Weekly, May 22.

Mohandas M (1992), Impact of New Settlers in the Western Ghat Region on the Socio-Economic Conditions of the Tribal Population-The Case Study of Wayanad District in Kerala, College of Co-Operation and Banking, Kerala Agricultural University, Thrissur.

Moorthy Narayana A, Jyotishi A and Deshpaande R.S. (1999), Agricultural Growth and Migration: Search for New Evidence, Indian Journal of Agricultural Economics, July-Sept.

Nair K S (1978), Ethnicity and Urbanisation, Ajantha Publications, New Delhi.

Nair Ramachandran K (1987), Utilisation of Foreign Remittance in Kerala, ICSSR Research Project, The Centre for Tropical Studies, Thiruvananthapuram.

Nambiar A C K (1995), The Socio-Economic Conditions of Gulf Migrants, Commonwealth Publishers, New Delhi.

Nayyar Deepak (1999), op.cit.

Ranis G and Fei J C H (1961), A Theory of Economic Development, American Economic Review, Sept.

Rao Lakshmana (1977), Internal Migration and Political Change in India, National Publishing House, New Delhi.

Ravenstein E G (1885), The Laws of Migration, Journal of Royal Statistical Society, Vol 48.

Rodriguez R Edward (1998), International Migration and Income Distribution in the Philippines, Economic Development and Cultural Change, No. 2, January.

Russel S and Teitelbaum M (1992), International Migration and International Trade, Discussion Paper No. 160, World Bank, Washington D C.

Sasikumar (1999), Theories of Internal Migration-A Critique of Neo-classical and New Economics of Migration, Labour and Development.

Singh Manjit (1997), Bonded Migrant Labour in Punjab Agriculture, Economic and Political Weekly, March 15.

Sovani (1966), Urbanisation and Urban India, Asia Publishing House, Bombay.

Stark Oded (1978), Economic Demographic Interactions in Agricultural Development- The Case of Rural Urban Migration, U.N Food and Agriculture Organisation, Rome.

Stark Oded (1983), A Note on Modeling Labour Migration in Less Developed Countries, The Journal of Development Studies, No. 4, July.

Stark Oded (1991), The Migration of Labour, Cambridge, Basil Blackwell.

Stark O Taylor E and Yitzhaki S (1986), Remittances and Inequality, Economic Journal (96).

Taylor E (1992), Remittances and Inequality Reconsidered: Direct Indirect and Intertemporal Effects, Journal of Policy Modeling, (14).

Taylor E J and Adelman I (1996), Migration and the Changing Structure of a Mexican Village Economy in Taylor E J and Adelman I (ed.), Village Economies- The Design, Estimation and Use of Village Wide Economic Models, Cambridge University Press, New York.

Tcha Moonjoong (1996), Altruism and Migration: Evidence from Korea and United States, Economic Development and Cultural Change, No.4.

Tharakan M (1978), Dimensions and Characteristics of the Migration of Farmers from Travancore to Malabar, 1930-50, Journal of Kerala Studies, June.

Todaro Michael P (1977), Economics for a Developing World, Longman.

Tripathy S N and Dash C R (1997), Migrant Labour in India, Discovery Publishing House, New Delhi.

United Nations (1953), Determinants and Consequences of World Population Trends, New York.

United Nations (1973), Determinants and Consequences of World Populations Trends, New York.

Upreti H C (1992), Impact of Migration on Development of Rural Kumaon, I C S S R Research Abstract Quarterly, No 1 and 2, Jan-June.

World Bank (1978), World Development Report, Washington.

Chapter 3

The Study Area, the People and their Early Life

This chapter gives a brief account about the village, the people and their life before the migration of people from Travancore. A better perspective on the migration associated socio-economic change can be made with this picture in the background. Before depicting the profile of the village and the early social and economic life of the people a brief mention may be made about the Malabar region and the Wayanad district to which the village belongs.

The Study Area

Malabar

The name Malabar spelt out variously as 'Malaibar', 'Mulibar' and 'Munibar' in medieval traveller's accounts appears to be the combination of two words – a Tamil Malayalam word 'malai' meaning hill and a Semitic word 'bar' meaning land. Originally it was not a political or administrative term but merely a geographical appellation. It must have included the entire West Coast but by the beginning of the age of European expansion in the 16th century it had come to be fixed in the present Kerala territory. Since the Maharashtra and Kerala portions were included in the powerful Vijayanagar Empire, the Mysore forces overran Kolathunadu and Kozhikode in the 18th century. The native rulers of Kerala organised resistance against this with the help of the English East India Company. However, by the end of the protracted struggle against Mysore, the Company, which posed as the saviour, had brought the northern parts of Kerala under their own rule. They did this by exploiting the weakness and the natural rivalries of many small principalities. The British revived the old name of Malabar and organised it into a district called British Malabar. Thus the region got distinguished from the southern region, which, were under the native dynasties of Cochin and Travancore. Gradually the prefix of British dropped out and Malabar survived as the name of the region comprising the present districts of Palakkad, Malappuram, Kozhikode, Wayanad, Kannur and Kasargod and a part of Thrissur. Today there is no political or administrative unit called Malabar. It is just a name.

Malabar has all the ingredients of a dreamland to people of all walks of life. To the nature lovers the majesty of the Western Ghats, radiant beauty of the blue seas with its white foam, green lagoons fringed with feathery palms and sparkling sand are marvellous to experience. So also the majestic mountain slops clad in dense forests and thick jungles nowhere else one can see. For the religious minded there are numerous temples like Thali and Lokanarkavu, which are adorned by sculptures and paintings. For the architect the traditional 'Thachushastra' of Malabar poses a challenge. For the aesthetically minded Malabar presents a variety of literatures from Kalaripayattu to the folklore of Vadakkan pattu. The region has several other striking features. It is Malabar from where the gold that bedecked Solomon's temple in the Halcyon days of Jewish sovereignty is said to have come. It is the province that gave birth to the boat building traditions of Beypore, which date back to the Sumerians and the Phoenicians. The folk art forms known as 'Theyyam' and 'Thirai' of Malabar go back to the Sangam age. Malabar witnessed many an event that changed the course of Indian history. It was Kappad- a pleasant calm beach studded with rocks and caressed by friendly waves- which turned a page in world history with the landing of Vasco-da- Gama. This is the Holy Land where history utters in sweet silence the glories of Kunhali Marakkar, one of the series of naval chiefs to stand up against Portuguese invasion. Pazhassi Raja who enthrals all patriots for his heroism was the proud son of Malabar. Another event that still lingers in the memory of the people is the historic 'Mamankam', the grand martial arts festival of the by gone era celebrated once in 12 years with splendour and gaiety. It was a historical event of the 10th century A.D showing the might and supremacy of the Zamorin, the ruler of erstwhile Malabar. The legend is that on these days the Zamorin will present himself on the main dais and the rulers of the small tiny states surrender the flags to him as a symbol of acceptance of the supremacy of the Zamorin. However, the ruler of Valluvanadu, a small princely state, never accepted the Zamorin's supremacy and sent warriors against the mighty army of Zamorin. They were known as Chavers or Suicide Squads. The king announces the conclusion of the mamankam after the Zamorin's brigade over powered the squad members. This is also the land of Kallai, which was once the second largest timber market in the world. It is in the banks of Feroke, that the ingenuous technical skill of man led to the making of tiles and bricks on factory scale. No doubt all these attractions inspired many of the foreign conquerors as well as the indigenous ones to bring the land under their control. Thus the Portuguese, the Dutch, the French, the British and Tippu Sultan craved to possess Malabar. Finally the British came to possess the land and ruled the region with Kozhikode as the capital of the region. The district was divided into four revenue divisions in addition to Fort Cochin. These four divisions were Thalassery, Kozhikode, Malappuram and Palakkad. After independence on the formation of the state of Kerala on November 1, 1956 the Malabar district was merged with the Travancore Cochin State by creating three districts such as Kozhikode, Kannur and Palakkad. Later, the three districts were further subdivided to form three more districts. Though integrated with the Travancore - Cochin state and governed for almost half a century by the native governments the region still stands separated from the rest of Kerala in terms of socio-economic development. A brief mention of this may now be made.

As mentioned above, the region covers six districts out of the 14 districts of Kerala extending to an area of 17463 sq. kms (44.93 percent) out of the 38863 sq. kms of the state. The region accounted for 41.56 percent of the total population of the State (120.94 lakhs out of 290.99 lakhs) in 1991 (Dept. of Economics and Statistics 1993:4). In the demographic composition Malabar accounted for 35.33 percent of total scheduled caste population and two fifths of total scheduled tribe population of the state (Dept of Economics and Statistics 1993: 6). While the general literacy level in the districts of Malabar are more or less comparable with the other districts of Kerala in most of the districts of Malabar the literacy rate among the SC/ST population stood lower than the other region. The infant mortality rate shown in Table 3.1 reveals that the probability of children to die was high in the Malabar region compared to the Travancore - Cochin area.

Table 3.1

Probability to die in Kerala before the age of five

Region	Age in years			
	1	2	3	4
Malabar	36.6	39.5	44.7	52.0
Travancore and Cochin	35.0	39.7	40.6	42.0

Source: Irudaya Rajan S and Mohanachandran P 1998 :1128.

On the economic front some of the features of the district makes distinct reading. In the occupational distribution of main workers it can be seen from Table 3.2 that the land based activities such as cultivation, agricultural work, livestocks and mining accounted for a higher share of workers, 50.95 percent. As against this the share of the other region was 46.17 percent. Trade and commerce too accounted for a large share in the Malabar region, 13.20 percent of total main workers against 12.28 percent recorded in the rest of the State. Within the land based activities it is significant to note that the proportion of agricultural labour was highest, 29.15 percent of the total work force while it was only 23.27 percent in the rest of Kerala.

Coming to the agricultural characteristics the average area of operational holding in the region was

Table 3.2

Occupational distribution of main workers in 1991 (in lakhs)

Category	Malabar	Percentage	Travancore-Cochin	Percentage
Cultivators	3.59	11.18	6.57	12.91
Agricultural labour	9.36	29.15	11.84	23.27
Livestock	2.90	9.03	4.77	9.38
Mining and quarrying	0.51	1.59	0.31	0.61
Household industry	0.55	1.71	1.59	3.12
Other than household industry	3.48	10.84	6.14	12.06
Construction	1.22	3.80	2.10	4.13
Trade and commerce	4.24	13.20	6.25	12.28
Transport and communication	1.92	5.98	3.03	5.96
Others	4.33	13.48	8.27	16.26
Total	**32.10**	**100.00**	**50.87**	**100.00**

Source: Dept. of Economics and Statistics 1993 :21.

0.38 ha. against 0.26 ha. in the Travancore - Cochin region in 1990-91 (Dept. of Economics and Statistics 1993: 44). The region has virtual monopoly position in the case of some of the crops (Table 3.3). Thus out of the total area devoted for sweet potato and coffee in the state Malabar claimed respectively 94 percent and 82.41 percent of the area. Similarly in the case of some of the other crops the region enjoyed dominance as 75.17 percent of the total area under cashew in the state, 59.69 percent of the area under tamarind, 59.48 percent of area under ginger, 56.53 percent of area under mango, 53.67 percent of area under jack and 53.54 percent of total area under pepper were in Malabar. In the case of the other important crops the position of the region is no less significant as 48.55 percent of the area under papaya, 47.58 percent of the area under turmeric, 47.17 percent of the area under paddy and 46.34 percent of the area under coconut are in the region (Table 3.3). At the same time the production statistics shown in the same table reveal that except few crops the productivity of crops is low in the region. The crops, which show higher yield are paddy, ginger, turmeric, cashew, jack fruits and mango. Even coffee in the case of which the region has virtual monopoly position the yield is low, as the share in production was 80.92 percent while the share of the area was 82.41 percent. Banana crop was also marked by low yield as with 50.81 percent of area the region contributes 32.42 percent of total output. Thus productivity of agriculture was less in the region compared to the Travancore- Cochin region.

Industrial development of the region also makes a similar reading (Table 3.4). While the share of the region in the total number of registered factories comes to 39.22 percent in employment the region's share was 22.25 percent. Also it can be discerned from the table that in the total number of registered small-scale industrial units the share of the region was less than a quarter. Besides in five out of the 6 districts of Malabar the per capita income stood far lower than the State average in 1992-93 (Dept. of Economics and Statistics 1993:332).

Table 3.3
Area and production of important crops

Crops	Area(ha) Malabar	State Total	Col.2 as% of col 3	Production (tonnes) Malabar	State Total	Col.5 as % of col.6
Paddy	263900	559450	47.17	519293	1086578	47.79
Pepper	90222	168507	53.54	22486	46802	48.04
Ginger	8412	14143	59.48	28199	45685	61.72
Turmeric	1270	2669	47.58	2505	5123	48.90
Banana	11229	22099	50.81	63793	196790	32.42
Cashewnut	86909	115621	75.17	85122	102771	82.83
Jack	38107	71002	53.67	147344	266043	55.38
Mango	42673	75480	56.53	181975	241054	75.49
Tamarind	8953	14999	59.69	19079	36441	52.36
Sweet potato	2447	2603	94.00	-	-	-
Papaya	6159	12685	48.55	26954	55999	48.13
Coconut	403197	870022	46.34	1906	4232	45.03
Coffee	61856	75057	82.41	16920	20910	80.92

Source: Dept. of Economics and Statistics 1993: 47-68.

Table 3.4

Indicators of industrial development

Indicators	Malabar	Percentage	Travancore-Cochin	Total
No of registered working factories (1992)	5470	39.22	8476	13946
Employment (1992)	090280	22.25	315558	405838
No of registered SSI units (1992)	2828	24.78	8583	11411

Source: Dept. of Economics and Statistics 1993: 108-111.

Infrastructure is also less developed in the region. Some of the indicators shown in Table 3.5 reveal this. While in the Malabar region road length per sq. km comes to 0.44km. in 1992-93 it was 0.61km. in the Travancore-Cochin area. As against one post office per

Table 3.5

Indicators of transport and communication development

Items	Malabar	Travancore-Cochin
Road length per sq. km (92-93)	0.44	0.61
Population per post office (1993)	5823	5800
Population per telephone connection (1994)	93	56

Source: Dept. of Economics and Statistics 1993: 197-212.

5823 persons in Malabar in the other region of Kerala it was per 5800 persons. In 1994 while in Malabar there was one telephone connection per 93 persons it was per 56 persons in the case of the other region. Facilities for education particularly higher education are also less developed in the region (Table 3.6). While in the case of lower primary and upper primary education there were more developed facilities in the case of facilities for high school education the region is less favourably placed. Accordingly, while in the Travancore-Cochin region there was 1 high school per 10092 persons in Malabar it was 1 high school per 15309 persons. Availability of facilities for higher education is also not different as the population size per Arts and Science College was 140537 in the rest of Kerala and 232576 in Malabar. Thus altogether it appears that the region is less developed socially and economically.

Table 3.6

Indicators of social infrastructure development

	Population per school/college/medical insitution	
Items	Malabar	Travancore-Cochin
Schools in 93-94		
Lower primary	2212	2565
Upper primary	8255	11695
High school	15309	10092
Arts and science colleges in 92-93	232576	140537
No. of medical institutions in 92-93	23667	23326

Source: Dept. of Economics and Statistics 1993: 218-240.

Wayanad

On the formation of the state Wayanad was divided into North Wayanad and South Wayanad which belonged to the Kannur and Kozhikode districts respectively. Later on 1st Nov. 1980 when the districts were reorganised the North and South Wayanad were merged to form the Wayanad district, which became the 12th district of Kerala. Wayanad is denoted variously as 'Vananadu' (forest land) and 'Vayalnadu' (paddy land). The district is situated at a distance of 76 kms. from the seashore of Kozhikode in the Western Ghats. Wayanad is also known as the Kashmir of Kerala known for its cold, salubrious climate. The main land route connecting Kozhikode with some of the important South Indian tourist centres of Mysore, Ootty and Bangalore pass through Waynad. The whole of the district is high land area placed between 700 and 2100 meters above the sea level. The district has a total land area of 2132 sq. kms (5.49 percent of the area of the state). Wayand with a total forest area of 78787 ha. accounts for 37.07 percent of the total forest area of the state. In the total cropped area of 1.13 lakh ha. 63 percent of the area is devoted for plantation i.e. 64469 ha. The hills are contiguous to Mudumalai in Tamil Nadu and Bandipur in Karnataka thus forming a vast landmass for the wild life to dwell in its natural abode. It is the natural beauty of Wayanad, which led Sir. M.E. Grant Duff the former Governor of Madras to remark " had Wayanad been in Europe, it would have become the favourite hunt of the landscape painters and views from it would have adorned every art gallery"(Malabar Mahotsav Committee 1994:232).

Historians are of the view that organised human life existed in this part at least 10 centuries before Christ. Traces of New Stone Age civilization have been discovered from various parts of Wayanad. The Edakkal cave situated on the summit of the Ambukuthi mala, which is just 3 kms. away from the little town of Ambalavayal has myriad engravings and epigraphs incised on the cave walls, which are believed to be the contributions of people, lived in the neo lithic period. Historians are of the view that it is the only one of its kind in the whole of South India testifying the presence of Stone Age man. Some of the historical evidences collected from various sources from the district indicate that agricultural practices in Wayanad were as old as 384 centuries before or after the beginning of the Christian era. It was an important trading centre as it connected the plain lands of Kerala in the West, East of Tamil Nadu and Karnataka. Ivory, forest products, spices like pepper, cardamom and ginger were the important products exported from the area. The region was known among the Europeans, Arabs and Egyptians for pepper with medicinal value. Thus the area had trade contact with other countries quite early. It was also found that Wayanad was a place of Sangamam (confluence). Evidences in the form of Veerakkal found on the way leading to some of the places testify this. Travel was very risky during the period and hence traders and others used to travel with bodyguards. As some of them died on the way while defending their masters in their memory stones were laid known as Veerakkal.

The Jains who believed in Ahimsa too established their abode in Wayanad when in the middle ages the Jains were subjected to harassment. It was said that their first migration must have taken place from Sravana Balagola an important Jain centre in the South. They penetrated in to the region through the territories of Mysore and Tamil Nadu. The features of Wayanad were ideal for them to stay uninfluenced by external forces. Thus came up many Jain temples in Waynad. While in other parts of Kerala Jains lost their identity and was wiped out completely at the influx of Hinduism, in Wayanad their presence continued.

In the ancient days this part was ruled by the Rajas of the Veda tribe. Later Wayanad came under the rule of Pazhassi Raja of Kottyam royal dynasty. It is recorded that it was Pazhassi who laid down effective measures for the administration and development of agriculture of the district. Several Nair families were brought into this forest land from the coastal region. They were given administrative responsibility as feudal Lords of the area. Their relationship with their former villages was eliminated by a separate declaration of the Raja. In this way Wayanad became populated. Thus it is also concluded that it was Pazhassi Raja who initiated the first wave of migration. The families who were thus brought to Wayanad were known as Kuppathodu Nair, Kalpetta Nair, Thariodu Nair, Eleppanna Nair, Varayal Nair and Pemoth Nambiar. They were made Deshavazhis (local rulers) of the respective villages, and in the feudal pattern were known with the title of their jurisdiction.

After the fall of Pazhassi Raja the British confiscated the land properties of the allies of Pazhassi Raja. Thus the private land holdings were converted into government land and sold to British capitalists. The entry of British also opened up the way for the onset of modern civilization. The isolation of Wayanad from the rest of the region was done away with the development of transport and communication. Roads were laid across the dangerous slopes of Wayand from Kozhikode and Thalassery. Those roads were extended to the city of Mysore and Ootty through Gudalore. Plantation of coffee, tea, pepper, cardamom etc. developed on the virgin lands in a more organised form. Many of the tribes and other communities who were dispossessed of land also became a source of cheap labour supply to the plantation companies

One of the prominent features of Wayanad is a variety of scheduled tribes are concentrated in the district. They consist of various sects like Paniyas, Kurumars, Adiyas, Kuriachias, Ooralis, Kattunaikans etc.

Pulpally-The Study Village

Pulpally village is situated in the interior of the Wayanad district and is also far off from the important main land routes of Wayanad such as the Kalpetta - Mysore road and Kalpetta- Kannur road. The village is about 50 kms away from the Kalpetta town, the district headquarter of Wayanad. It forms part of the Sultan Battery Taluk. Covering an area of 7675.36 ha (18958.13 acres) the village is located adjacent to Karnataka on the banks of the Kabini River in the North. The other three sides of the village are surrounded by reserve forests and on the East comes the Patichira village, West the Nadavayal village and in the South the Poothadi village. The Patichira village formed in 1983, was carved out of the Pulpally village. Though Pulpally is located on the North East of the Wayanad district and possess all the geographical features of the Western Ghats it is situated lower than the altitude of other areas of Wayanad district. Hence the climate of Pulpally is slightly different from the rest of Wayanad.

As per the village records the village has two divisions, Pakkam covering an area of 4762.04 ha. and Pulpally covering and area of 2913.31 ha. Most of the land in the village belonged to the Pulpally Temple (devaswom) before migration. A part of the land is reserve forests. Out of the total area of 7675.36 ha 3155.91 ha (41.12 percent) of the area of the village is reserve forest. As to the agricultural operations pepper is the main plantation crop. At the same time other crops are also grown in the village. Irrigation is less developed in the village as the 5 lift irrigation projects covers an area of 99.0422 ha out of a 3611.3384 ha. possession (2.74 percent of area).

As per the 1991 population census the village has a population of 25812 persons comprising of 12017 females and 13795 males. This gives a sex ratio of 871 females per 1000 males. Out of the total population 4307 were the tribes (16.68 percent). The sex ratio of tribal population appears as distinct as there were 906 females per 1000 males. In the village there were 71 tribal colonies with 817 houses.

The place has intimate connection with the Ramayana epic as several places in the village are said to have witnessed some of the events in the Ramayana. It is believed that when Sita Devi pleaded with her mother to recall her the land got divided engulfing her into depths. The hair got separated from the head before the entry. Thus the place which, got the name Jatayatta Kavu is in Pulpally. Sasimala of Pulpally is supposed to be the place where Lava and Kusa played in their childhood. Ashramakolli, which is another place in Pulpally, is believed to be the place where Valmiki's ashram was situated. Another legend also strengthens this story and it is related to the absence of leech in Pulpally while in other areas of Wayanad it is a serious menace. The story runs thus. One morning Valmiki noticed blood stains on the leg of Sita Devi due to the bite of leech. The Maharshi cursed the worm and thereupon it become extinct in the area once for all. The river flowing through the village called Kannarampuzha, which is also known as Kannunirpuzha, is said to have formed out of the tears of Sita Devi. There is also a temple with Sita, Lava and Kusa as the deities. It is the oldest and the most important temple of the village. This temple owned most of the land of the Pulpally village in the old days. It was also from Pulpally that a place called Thazhekavu that a shila writing, one of the oldest relics found from Wayanad was unearthed. When an old temple was destroyed between 100-150 Christ years the group called Nalpathiyennayiravar as offering reconstructed the temple and the town as per the relic. Thus the village has much historical importance right from the epic period.

The land also witnessed several other important events later. Most important of all was the death of Pazhassi Raja. In the end of the 18th century and the beginning of the 19th century there was revolt against the British in the region of Malabar and the Kerala Varma Pazhassi Raja provided the leadership. One of his main camps was in Pulpally at the Sita Devi Temple where he used to worship and stay. He was also able to get the overwhelming support from the local people including the tribes in nis guerrilla fight against the British. In an encounter with the British army led by Mr. T H Babelar, the then Malabar district Collector, Pazhassi Raja rather than accepting defeat did atmarpanam (self-dedication) at Mappilathodu at Pulpally situated very close to the Mysore forest on 30th November 1805. It is also believed that his own men had betrayed him. A memorial for him is being constructed at the site by the Pulpally panchayat. Pulpally also witnessed the attack of Tippu and the remnants of the bridge which was constructed on the Kannanarampuzha can still be found in the village. He also constructed a road towards Mysore.

The village has natural attraction and potential for tourism development. The Kuruva dweep with seven streams and a number of thuruthukal (twists) situated by the side of the forest is one such nature's gift. The forests surrounding the three sides of the village have rich wild life and rare herbal plants.

The People and their Early Social and Economic Life

Migration has brought about significant changes in the village. In fact the migrants outnumbered the locals. Thus on the existing social, cultural and economic life came new influences. The impact was also all pervading, as there occurred a process of metamorphosis in the social, economic, cultural and political life of the people. All the more important was the transformation of the village economy. From a primitive state the economy of the village witnessed an unparalleled all round development. The main architects were also the migrants. Before depicting a perspective on this let us have a look at the pre-migration social and economic life of the people and the village economy in general as the dynamics of migration associated change can be viewed in a better perspective in this background. The following paragraphs portray the early social and economic life of the people of the Pulpally village and the characteristics of the village economy at the time of migration.

The People

Based on some of the tools such as kalluli, kanmazhu kandabaranangal and shila pictures unearthed from the village historians have come to the conclusion that there was human habitation in the village as early as recorded history. The place was also recorded as thickly populated. Some of the later developments however forced many people to leave the village. As mentioned in the preceding section Pulpally was one of the main camps of Pazhassi Raja and he fought his last battle against the British at Pulpally. With the death of Pazhassi Raja the British started harassing the tribes and other communities for having joined with the Raja in the war against the British. Cultivation of forestland was also forbidden and land revenue was steeply hiked. Non payment of revenue also meant auction of the land and hence many of the communities got alienated from the land. Unable to withstand the situation many left the village. Thus at the time of migration only in certain pockets of Pulpally there was human habitation. It was also a Uni - Religious Hindu settlement. The inhabitants belonged to broadly two Hindu sects i.e. the tribes and non-tribes. The non-tribes were mainly the Chetties and Gowdas who is said to have migrated to the place about 400 years ago from the border state of Karnataka and Tamil Nadu. They also believe that they were adopted by the temple in the old days for the purpose of certain temple duties. There are three categories of Chetties in the area such as the Wayanadan, Elanadan, and Mountadan. Most of the Chetty settlements were in Pakkam, Chekadi and Pulpally. They have a language of their own which is somewhat identical to Kannada. They are chiefly cultivators and led a settled life. The scheduled tribes consisted of various communities such as the Paniyas, Naikans, Kurmars and Ooralis.

The Social Structure

The Indian social structure was complex and it varied from region to region. In the village though the traditional practices were more rigid migration introduced radical changes and hence mention may be made of the social structure and practices. The social structure we illustrate with reference to the institutions of religion/caste, economy, kinship and marriage. As is usual a hierarchical social structure existed in the village. As goes our observation there was only one Brahmin family settled in Chekady and hardly there was any Nair family in Pulpally at the time of migration. In fact the Kuppathodu Nair Tharavadu, which owned and managed the Pulpally Sita Devi temple was settled at Panamaram located about 13 kms away from Pulpally. There were no scheduled castes in the village. Thus the community comprised of a Brahmin household, Chetty/Gowda and tribal households. In this the Brahmin was placed at the top of the social structure and the tribal at the lower end. Untouchability was very much in practice. While the Chetties and tribes were untouchable to the Brahmins the tribes were untouchable to the Chetties. Untouchability was so rigid that the untouchables were not allowed to enter even on the veranda of the house. Even the children of Chetty households were not allowed to play with the untouchables and if played they had to take bath before entering the house. Also if one went out of the household surroundings only after taking bath they can enter the house. Food is served to tribal people in open place outside the house in a pit covered with the banana leaf. Even on festival occasions this was practiced. Water drawing by the polluted was strictly prohibited.

Within the community there was caste distinction. Though the various denominations of Chetties and Gowdas mingled and shared food matrimonial alliance was strictly prohibited. Among the tribal population the system was much more rigid. In the hierarchy on the top was the Kurumars and in the bottom Paniyas/ Adiyas. They do not mingle with each other. To state within the same community even on friendly visits food was not shared from the house and the guests prepared themselves and ate. Within the family too there existed discrimination. Among the Chetty households the joint family system with Marumakkathayam was prevalent. The head of the household called the Karanavar was supreme and his decisions were final. To mention the extent of supremacy, even on some petty reasons if the Karanavar comes to conclude that the matrimonial alliance of the dependent person should be severed even if his decision is unreasonable it has to be done. The Karanavar always has to be respected by touching the feet. The status was conferred hereditary and the oldest in the family becomes the Karanavar. The properties were looked after and managed by the Karanavar. So also he managed the household affairs. The Karanavar and his wife used to enjoy a high status in the family. In living conditions and in the provision of food and cloth this was clearly manifested as while the Karanavar and his wife lived lavishly others were provided with bare minimum for their living. Thus the status of dependents was one of subordinate and some times equivalent to slaves. At the same time wealth accumulation resulted in the form of money, jewellery and grain among the Chetty households. Monetary and gold savings in those days were kept in a box and hidden in the land known only to the Karanavar. As no one in the family will have an idea about the size of savings and its whereabouts on the unexpected death of the Karanavar the savings usually get lost. No surprise from some of the disposed land such savings were later realised by the new owners including the migrants. Women were strictly confined to kitchen work.

Each tribe had also its headman. For e.g. each Paniya settlement had a headman called Kuttan appointed by the landlord. In rank to Kuttan was the Mudali or head of the family. Both Kuttan and Mudali are called Mooppan. The Chieftains under whom the Paniyas worked also appointed Chemmi the so-called priest of the Paniyas in olden days. The office was hereditary and in the absence of hereditary Chemmi it could be filled up by election. Monogamy appears to be the general rule among the Paniyas. The Paniyas have only a crude idea of religion. Their major deity is called Kali who is believed to be malignant and powerful. They also worship Banyan tree. Thus they hesitate to cut the Banyan tree and if cut it is believed that he would fall sick. Paniyas constituted the main agricultural labour force and are also engaged in all the works outside the home of Chetties. It was more or less a feudalistic set up in which the Paniyas were the slaves and the Chetites the cultivators.

Kattunaikans are primitive tribes mainly dependent on forest products. They are also known as Then Kurumar (Honey Kurumar) since they collect honey and other forest products. The physical appearance of the community was that of hill tribe. They seldom mingle with other communities. The sect has also a headman called Muttan whose decisions are said as final. Kattunaikans worship animals, birds, trees, rocks, hillocks, snakes etc. They are firm believers in black magic and sorcery. Apart from the worship of Hindu deities such as Vishnu, Siva and Bhagavathy they also worship the ancestors. In each family there was a small temple.

Language differed among the various communities. Kattunaikan's language is an admixture of all the Dravidian languages. Chetties spoke a scriptless language, similar to Kannada. Even now they speak this language at home.

There was diversity in the custom of marriage among the communities. Some of the peculiar features may be mentioned. Among the Chetties there was no dowry system where as bride price has to be paid. For the fixation of marriage the bride has to come with ornaments (mostly silver) and it is not obligatory on the part of the bride to have ornaments. On marriage the relation of the girl is totally severed with the family. It was so rigid that it is called Pulayozhivakkal (funeral ablution). It was also widely prevalent that on the death of the elder brother the younger brother marries the sister in law if she is younger to him and fertile. Also it was the right of a person to marry the Karanavar's daughter. Marriage is held at the bridegroom's house. The bride and the party reach the day before the marriage and camp in the house of the bridegroom. The custom is to have a pandhal (shed) with 12 poles. The first pole called muhurthakkal (auspicious pole) is placed after performing a ritual called Daivamkanal (God seeing). The Velichappad performs this and cites the place. In the pit a thin piece of gold is placed and the muhurthakkar (auspicious persons) who are the velichappad, the bridegroom and his parents fix the muhurthakkal. Cultural programmes of kolkali and vattakali used to be performed during the occasion. The bride and the bridegroom dress like Parvathi and Parameswara. All the relatives gather in the house for seven days in advance for the marriage. The expense was so heavy that households get impoverished with a marriage.

Where as among Ooralis the custom was simple and inexpensive. The groom's family brings paan and it is distributed among the invitees after the marriage. In marriage the Mooppan has an important role. Once the parents finalises an alliance the proposal is placed before the Mooppan. He convenes a meeting of all the people of the colony and on discussion their permission is sought. Liquors are served. The custom is to tie a yarn with gold locket on the neck of the bride. The bride and the bridegroom wear all the ornaments in the colony. Then there is a custom of drawing water. About 50 females and the bride assemble near the well. The bride draws a pot of water and goes to the husband's house accompanied by a group of women. The Karanavathi (the bridegroom's mother) prevent the bride in the varandha. The bride then offers paan and presentations to the Karanavathi. Karanavathi can put any questions and the bride has to answer and then only she is admitted to the house. Among the Paniyas from the day of fixation of marriage to the date of marriage household provisions has to be supplied to the bride by the bridegroom.

All communities had good faith in God. Manthravadam (sorcery) was common. If a household has any problem a pooja called Daivamkanal is performed. The Velichappad performs it. For each community there was a Velichappad. In front of the Daivapura (family temple) the Velichappad dances in tune with the songs and music. It is believed that at the climax the soul of the ancestors enters into him and he suggests the remedy. Even in acute illness the Pooja is performed as a remedy. The Velichappad even predicts whether the sick will survive or die. In cases of survival prescriptions are also given by him. This is considered as final as no other treatment is available.

With every death in the household the Paniyas shift the house.

The Landscape and the Settlement Pattern

Though situated in the highland the landscape of the village was more or less typical of other plain lands of Kerala. There are small hills. At the end of some of the hill slopes flow streams quite small and big. They are followed by plain paddy fields. Thus in between two hills lie the paddy fields. Some of the streams flow through the middle of the paddy fields. In the case of others the hills are continuous and in between the two hill slopes flow the streams. The settlement pattern of various communities has certain features. The Chetty households are scattered and located at the lower end of the hill slopes very close to the paddy field. Leaving a part of the garden land developed for cultivation of other subsistence crops the other sides of the houses are surrounded by forests. The tribes are colonised and located at an audible distance from the houses of Chetties. The settlements are surrounded by forests on all sides. Each category of tribes have their exclusive pockets of settlement and they are cut off from each other. The tribes who depended on the forest for livelihood were settled in the further interior of the forest.

Each Chetty household will have a big cattle shed close to the house. They are thatched and fenced of bamboo. A separate thrown fenced shed is constructed for calf to protect them from tiger attack. During the summer season the cattle are kept in the paddy field with bamboo fencing. The place will be shifted frequently so as to spread the animal wastes all over the paddy field.

The Economy and the Livelihood System

The early life of the people of Pulpally was very primitive as subsistence cultivation and food gathering provided the main source of livelihood. Market dependence was minimum and thus it was more or less a low performing self-sufficient village economy. Thus some of the communities were specialised in the production of certain commodities and a system of exchange was conventionally evolved. Most of the essentials the Chetty households cultivated and the crops grown were paddy, orange, chilly, some tuber crops, coffee, elephant yam, tobacco, banana etc. The crops were grown for self-consumption and they were grown in the homestead. More or less shifting cultivation was practiced on garden land. All the inputs used were what was locally available. The genetic qualities of some of the seeds were however so poor that it took almost two years to draw yield. Paddy was cultivated as a single crop. Bio-fertilisers like cow dung, green leaves and ashes were abundantly used. The land was also so fertile that even the need for fertiliser was not felt for most of the crops. This was greatly supplemented by the rainwater, which carried ashes left out of the forest fire. Cultivation then was a gambling, as threat of wild animals like elephants, pigs, monkeys, wild boars etc. were constant. To protect the main crops night watch was maintained by erecting a small tent on the trees locally called erumatam, a tent on the tree. Noises are created frequently to drive away the wild animals. They were frightened with fire also. To meet the cash requirements and to purchase other essentials like salt, cloth etc. surplus products like banana, paddy, orange, ghee etc. were sold.

Though the tribes were also cultivators for generations their status slipped into slavery. The people who were brought from the plain lands and those favoured by the Britishers gained control of the land due to their accessibility to power. Hence the tribes were driven to slavery. Still some of the tribes practiced cultivation for self-consumption in the fringe of the forests. Such tribes mainly practiced shifting cultivation in the forest, as land was abundant. Ooralis specialised in making cane baskets, earthen pots and work tools. That was periodically made available to other communities and in return paddy and other products were bought. To those dependent upon the cultivators the essential commodities used to be provided by the cultivators.

Animal husbandry was another important source of livelihood. Only Chetties owned cattle. Cattle ownership was very extensive and this greatly supplemented the agricultural activities. It is said that some of the families possessed cattle up to 400. This was facilitated as there was extensive area including forest and the child/old aged labour force for tending cattle came from the tribal households. Milk and milk products thus used to be available in plenty. At the same time there was no market for milk. Surplus milk used to be washed away and as a practice the tribes are not served milk. In fact they were misled not to drink milk. Thus even if there were many milk cattle milk was drawn only from a few and the rest are allowed to be fed to the calf. The only dairy product that enjoyed the market was ghee, which used to be bought by the traders coming frequently. Ghee was lavishly consumed and was the main cooking oil. Food gathering was another important source of livelihood for the households. Hunting provided the meat. Many Chetties owned rifles. After the rainy season while the Chetties occasionally went for hunting the Mullakurumars regularly went for hunting. They went with arrow and bow tied to the waist carrying food packets escorted by dogs. The streams meandering through out the village provided abundant fish. Some of the forest products also became a source of livelihood. For e.g. the bamboo rice used to be cooked in and consumed by most of the households. The dependence of some of the tribes on the forest produce was almost total. Thus the common property resources played a significant role in sustaining the life of all. This was particularly true of some of the tribal households. Dependence on market was thus minimum in the day to day life of the people and was confined to the purchase of very essentials like cloth, salt, oil etc. Even for important functions like marriage, death etc. market dependence was less. It was customary on the part of the households mainly the neighbours and relatives to pool the grains, vegetables and other products for such functions. Some of the crops grown like elephant yam used to be harvested only on such special occasions.

Mention may also be made of the avenues of employment other than agriculture and food gathering. Elephant catching used to be organised by the temple authorities within their forestland. Elephant pits are dug by the Naikans and it is considered as their right. Daily wage is paid in the form of paddy by the temple authorities. The works are done under the overall supervision of the Muthali. When elephant gets drowned the Naikans stand guard day and night. The features of the elephant will be communicated to the temple authorities. A ritual will be performed in which the Velichappad will conclude whether the elephant has to be retained by the temple or set free. Raising the elephant from the pit and bringing it to the elephant camp is a celebration. Food will be prepared and served for about 200 persons involved in the process. A Thappana (trained elephant) also will be employed for the process. All the operations are done under the supervision of the Chetties. Even all the collection of ivory from the forest owned by the temple belonged to the temple. The only other employment was tree felling and its sizing.

Medical facilities of all type were non existent in the village. The nearest allopathic hospital was at Manantavady situated about 25 kms away. For most of the common ailments the indigenous herbal remedies known to the community was administered. Acute cases were only taken to the modern medical centres. Invariably the delivery was performed at home under the supervision of the experienced woman.

Malabar was under prohibition before migration. Still though not very widespread some of them were alcoholics. Among the Chetties Karanavars regularly drink. Even some of the Chetty ladies used to drink and smoke. They had the crude system to brew liquor out of paddy. Also toddy was tapped out of palm tree. All this was however done for self-consumption. Some used to purchase liquor from the neighbouring Mysore State. Tribes did not brew liquor and they sold paddy and purchased the liquor.

Washer and barber communities were missing in the village. Even mirror was said as not available and hence they mutually help in face shaving and hair cutting. As this was not regularly done they looked like jungle man.

The male adults wore half dhoti tied at the waist. Another half dhoti was used to cover above the waist.

Women wore a dhoti tied at the waist and a half dhoti is placed across the shoulder to cover the breast.

Thus the access to forest and the subsistence farming made this low-level economy to sustain on its own.

Transport, Communication and Trade

Contact with the outside world was less felt in the economy we depicted above. In the memory of the most aged person in the area none was employed outside the village. Hardly they went out of the village with family. The only occasion when the Chetties visited outside the village with family was to attend marriage. As plainly put by some of them the need for road was not felt by the people. Thus transport and communication facilities were practically non existent. The only mode of communication was the postal service and here again the beat postman visited Pulpally once in a week. Newspapers hardly reached the village and hence for all practical purposes they led an isolated life unaware of the happenings outside the village. The events of the village were also hardly known outside the village. On the market front shops selling even essentials were non existent not to speak of trading activities. The nearest market was at Panamaram (13 kms away). People had to traverse through the thick forest to reach Panamaram. When necessary they went in small groups to the town, purchased the essentials and transported on the head load of the tribes. The essentials were stocked for 3 to 6 months by the Chetty households. On head load called Thalachapu or Kotta periodically essentials including cloths used to be brought by few traders. They were mostly Muslims working as agents of merchants. In turn they bought the marketable products from the households. The chief items sold were paddy, banana, livestock products, goat, hen, calf, ghee etc. There was no standardised measurement and paddy used to be measured in hollow bamboo pieces. In the case of livestock and hen the purchaser sometimes left them with the households till a buyer was found. At the same time the traders retained the right over the off springs too if any. Till such time the households look after them and appropriate the income if any. It was not a cash economy as most of the transactions were made by exchange of goods.

Credit market as such can be said as non-existent. The lone financial institution was the Eikya Nanaya Sangom established in 1921. But for all practical purposes it was dormant. Most common form of lending was paddy. For every unit of borrowing almost two units has to be repaid in the next season as per the prevalent rate. The workers used to borrow from the cultivators regularly and the cultivators in times of distress borrow from the traders based in Panamaram. It was repaid in paddy at the above-mentioned exorbitant rate.

Education

Educational development depends on a number of factors. The perception of the population about education, the accessibility to education, the affordability and the scope for reaping the benefits of education are some of the important factors. On most of these counts there was less conducive an environment for educational development. As far as educational facilities were concerned as early as 1924 at the initiative of the Church of South India (CSI) a lower primary school was established at Chekady, which was one of the early settlement of the Chetties and tribes. We have been told that it was with the intention to convert the locals to Christianity that the institution was established by the Missionaries. In 1939 due to shortage of students the recognition of the school was withdrawn. Later the Malabar District Board gave recognition and since then it functioned as a government school. In 1948 an elementary school was established at Pulpally. Its origin dated back to 1938 as inspired by the then Harijan Upliftment Programme of the Indian National Congress Sri Kuppathodu Madhavan Nair the then Devaswom Manager started the school to impart literacy to the tribal population. Later as the Congress Committee faced difficulty in running the school the Manager in his personal capacity managed the school. It was known as United Aided Elementary School. Getting teachers was then difficult. Somehow he managed the problems. Thus these two schools constituted the formal facilities for the school education in the village. Even though facilities came up peripherally they remained inaccessible as even the grown up males hardly dared to go alone through the forest not to speak of sending the children. The perception of the people is also a factor that has to be reckoned with. Employment outside agriculture was unheard of as there was little interaction with the outside world. A strong perception also prevailed among them against education and other employment. In the perception of Chetties the boys were an object to carry out the agricultural operations. Hence they were trained for the agricultural practices at a very early age. In the case of girls the outlook was much more conservative that they have to be trained as housewives. Thus an early wedlock was arranged. It was also believed that girls become immoral if educated. In the case of the tribes it was also a widely prevalent belief that if educated they may have to compulsorily go for military or police service which they cannot think of. Thus apart from poor development of educational facilities the outlook of the people was also conservative. Those who were somewhat receptive arranged basic education to their wards by arranging the ezhuthasan (Teacher) at home. They were provided accommodation and food. Thus a few joined together and shared the cost. Food was provided in rotation by the participating households. A fee was also collected from the participating households and paid to him. Very few wealthy Chetties sent the children to boarding schools for education. Here it may be mentioned that one of the highest educated was a Chetty who studied for graduation at Thalassery. He too took up the ancestoral job. As per our observation though he was offered a job in the forest department he declined to accept the same as his grand father felt the job of protecting the forest as demeaning in nature. This well speaks about the conservatism of the people.

Agrarian System and the Agrarian Relations

The agrarian structure of the village differed a little from the rest of the state as land ownership was concentrated and there was the prevalence of the tenancy system. Feudalistic practices too were there. Most of the land belonged to the devaswom. On the death of Pazhassi the temple and the assets mainly land to the extent of about 20000 acres (at the time of land reform measures as per records there were 14998.08 acres) went to the Kuppathodu tharavadu, which was one of the oldest Nair family of Wayanad based at Panamaram. They were managing the temple and the land. Individual Janmies (land owners) also held a few pockets of land and some area was owned as forests by the government. Cultivation was on lease basis for which pattom (rent) had to be paid annually. Revenue land was also made available for cultivation up to 5 acres either on rent or Janmam (with ownership title). For janmam lands as a lump sum amount has to be paid most of the cultivators took land on rental basis. Size of paddy land is reckoned with reference to the size of seed sown. In the Chekady area most of the landholdings were Janmam. While Chetties were the cultivators the tribal sects in particular the Paniyas were the agricultural labour. The system in practice was more or less equivalent to slavery. Thus most of the tribal families were permanently attached with the Chetty households. They work through out the year in the farm and houses of the cultivators. The children, the old and disabled go for tending cattle. They were also engaged in driving away the monkeys from the agricultural fields. The agricultural operations mainly confined to paddy cultivation and work in orange farm. Hence the workers had very narrow job specialisation. The cultivators used to exercise masterly right over the workers and hence they were subjected to inhuman treatment. In farm seasons even the sick labour was forced to work. While some provided daytime food others provided paddy. The hardship of the labour was such that when paid in the form of paddy they had to process the paddy instantly and cook. After taking food they had to be present for the afternoon work. Here it is important to note that the productivity of labour was given no consideration in the system. In accordance with the feudal practice the labour was also employed up to the zero marginal product. In the case of other tribes while men went for hunting and gathering forest products females went for the agricultural work. Some of the males of the sect also worked with the cultivators and their job was to drive away the monkeys and to tend cattle. The prevalent payment system was daily wages. The labour was also entitled to a portion of the yield from the paddy field. Usually the boundary line yield belonged to them. Later on this entitlement got sizably reduced. To tribes on unemployed days were paid half the daily wage. Apart from daily wage the permanent labour was given extra paddy on festival days in addition to the provision of half bottle oil, paan, tobacco, areca nut, coconut and jaggery. Further on Onam (a festival of Kerala) cloths are also provided to the labour. At the time of the temple festival they are entitled to some amount of cash. In passing a particular type of agricultural operation for separating the paddy from the stalk may be mentioned which is called Okkal. A pole will be fixed and few cattle will be tied to it. On ground the paddy bundles will be spread after unbundling. The cattle will be driven on them in rounds to separate the grain from the stalk. Once certain rounds are completed the paddy will be collected and the balance remaining with the stalk is given to the labour as kind payment.

Many cultivators owned bullocks. She buffaloes were also employed for the agricultural operations. The practice of others was to hire the pair on an annual basis, as some of the cultivators owned more than a pair of bullocks. Thus at the beginning of the season i.e. April/ May months the bullocks are hired and by January they are returned to the owner. The animals have to be maintained by the lessee. The tenant cultivators are under an obligation to render free bullock and labour power to the land operated by the Janmies directly. Thus they have to go with all the labour at their disposal and work tools to the field of the Janmy at the sowing season, prepare the field and sow.

As stated above the agricultural labourers were more or less slaves. It was customary too and was known as Wayanadan slavery. Locally the practice was also called Valliyurkavu panam or Niravu panam. Valliyurkavu is one of the famous temples in the Wayanad district. The annual festival lasting for 14 days begins on 1st of Meenam (usually March). Most of the people participate in the celebration and a system of exchange of tribal agriculture labour takes place. For one year by paying the Atimapanam (slave money) the cultivators enters in to an oral contract. The ruling wage has to be paid. The then prevailing slave price was for married man Rs. 10 and women Rs.5. For one year they are obliged to work with the person paying the Atimapanam. The labour is paid daily wage at the prevailing rate. The contract is strictly followed as the deal is made before the Kavilamma (Goddess). The system was widely prevalent among some of the tribes like, Paniyas, Adiyas, Naikans, and Kurumars etc. Even if the contract is not made in the temple the system is that the labour has to be paid the Atimapanam annually by the cultivator at the time of the temple festival. Otherwise the labour will accept atimapanam from other cultivators and shift.

On the whole it can be seen that there was a social system for the distribution of the produce. Though the distribution was uneven it provided the necessary means for the dependants to survive.

Living Conditions

The housing and other facilities for living for all categories of people were very pitiable. Reasonably built houses had mud walls. The practice was to prepare mud paste with the help of cattle and to erect the wall by just placing the mud in the same form for almost two feet width. Thus walls are erected. Top is thatched with paddy stalk on a frame made of bamboo. Height of the wall is almost 6/7 feet. Sometimes ceiling is made for which large sized woods are shaped and placed horizontally and vertically. On it a bamboo frame is placed and mud flooring is given. The walls are carved, made plain and painted with some kind of red soil. Sometimes even pictures are drawn on the wall. There will be two openings one at the front and the other at the backside. Sized wood is used for the door with country locking system. Even two storied houses are constructed so by the Chetties. At the same time most of the other houses are made of bamboo. Even the house was synonymous with bamboo forest. The usual practice was to weave the cane (by tying) and keep it erect by planting on the earth. Mud is then pasted on it thickly and this constitutes the wall. This is to give some protection from severe cold. Roof is thatched with the palm leaf or hay on bamboo frame. The floor was invariably cow dung pasted. The doors and coats are also made of bamboo. Most of the houses were of this type. The tribal houses were invariably of this type. The houses are constructed 5 to 6 feet above the ground level as a protection against the attack of wild animals.

As to the availability of other facilities though water was abundantly available in the area none owned wells of the modern type. Even in small pits water was plenty. For all purposes hot water was used. Even river water was then clean to drink.

Weather was so bitterly cool that people used to sleep near the fire. The climate was such that due to mist sunshine becomes visible only by 11 a.m. Lighting by the tribes were with firewood. Most of the Chetties used kerosene lamp. For almost 9 months it used to rain with 3 months of intensive rain. As mentioned, some of them used to reckon the months by the change of climate. Accordingly when the monsoon sets in they reckon the month as etavam (May/June) and at the onset of misty season as vrichikam (October/November). Implicit in this was the fact that monsoon never failed in the old days.

Social Life and Customary Practices

The people of all communities had their own entertainment and festivals. In the case of Chetties the entertainment was kolkali and vattakkali. There are not many occasions when people of different castes will congregate. One is the temple festival. There are customary rights and responsibilities to each community. For festival the forests surrounding the temple will be cleared and pandhal (shed) will be erected. The organisational responsibility for the festival was with three chetty families of Eriapplly, Yogimoola and Etamala. Each caste has its own responsibility. Thus clearing of forests, construction of pandhal, supply of wood, supply of cane baskets, collection of banana leaf for serving food, cleaning of vessels, cutting of vegetables etc. are assigned to each community. The Brahmins prepare the feast and food is served to each community separately in order of their social status. The administration was by the Kuppathodu tharavadu. On 20th Dhanu (falling in December/January) with Vellat (a ritual) the festival begins. Customarily a representative of the Kuppathodu tharavadu and Etamala, Eriappally, Yogimoola Sthanik Chetties, Kondamala, Kurichipatta Mooppan, Matappally,

Etamala, Mathils has to participate in the function. All the tenants have to offer rice for the temple festival. Rice measurement done on 18th Dhanu is also an important function. As per the custom the Etamala or Eriappally Chettie's rice is being measured by a member of Kuppathodu tharavadu and placed in a bamboo box. Yogimoola Chetties are the custodian of the hundi. Adivasi Naikans and Mullakurumars have special status and rights. Vessels and lamps are brought from the Tharavadu. The trustee also has to be brought from Panamaram escorted by two persons. When he reaches the temple he has to be received by salute guns. Community feast is arranged on the last day of the celebration. On the seventh day a ritual is practiced at the Valmiki ashram. The Naikans will reconstruct the roof with the poa grass (dharba pullu) and it is believed that the next day they would get wild buffalo or a swan. During the festival days all of them gather together sing, dance eat and enjoys. It was also the only occasion on which all the goods are made available to the people of the village as market called Chanda (market) used to be organised. The tribes find the occasion as an opportunity to spend their cash earnings. Their list of annual purchase include brass bangles, muthu-mukkuthi (ear and nose wearing), paan bags, readymade dresses, rice bran, pea nuts etc. Without distinction they sing, dance in tune to the flute and go around. A number of their traditional arts are performed. The old sit around the fire and chat. This was the occasion one forgets all the worries.

The only other occasion on which all the males congregate is to lead the elephant from the pit when an elephant is caught. As mentioned it is like a festival in the village.

When elephants are spotted in the vicinity they offer coconut and rice bran. Also it was customary that when a lion is killed its body has to be brought before the janmy (the land owner). He places a piece of cloth and money on the body and the same belongs to the killer.

On the whole to conclude though the village was in an underdeveloped state life was peaceful. There was no robbery and crimes were unheard of.

REFERENCES

Dept. of Economis and Statistics (1993), Statistics for Planning, Govt. of Kerala, Trivandrum.

Irudaya Rajan S and Mohanachandran P (1998), Infant and Child Mortality Estimates- Part I, Economic and Political Weekly, May 9-15.

Malabar Maholtsav Committee (1994), Malabar-Souvenir, Kozhikode.

Chapter 4

Pulpally—The Flow of Settlers

The flow of peasants from the middle and southern part of Kerala in search of fertile cultivable land and permanent settlement in the northern part of Kerala started since 1920's. While a few settled on plain lands many moved to high ranges. Settlements were also close to the forests where cost of land was low and scope for encroachment was high. Wayanad district was most favourably placed and hence attracted many of them. Thus largest migration was also to the Wayanad district. At the same time it was also true that migration to Wayanad was a wild dream in their minds. On the one side there was the threat of wild animals and on the other side diseases like malaria took a heavy toll of human lives. Social and other physical infrastructure facilities were poorly developed not to speak of the availability of other basic conditions for living. The climate was also most inhospitable to them. The primitive nature of the living of the people depicted above which is more or less true of all Wayanad villages are further illustrative of the quality of life of the people. Thus life was a real challenge and the hard realities they encountered in the initial phase of migration are little known outside. This chapter makes an attempt to portray the hardships the migrants faced in the initial years and the strategies adopted by them to cope up with the situation in the host place. As a prelude to this an attempt is also made to put the migration process in a historical perspective and the characteristics of the migrants.

Travancore Migration-The History, Causes and Its Features

Origin of Travancore Migration

Historical evidences indicates that migration of peasants from Travancore started from the early twenties of the last century. The source of this migration was dominantly the Travancore, the southern region of the present Kerala State. They settled down not only within the Malabar district but also in the border areas of the then Mysore and Tamil Nadu States. In fact the first one migrated to Mysore. It was Mr. Avira Tharakan Ezhupunna Parayil from Shertallai, a low land taluk of Travancore (Tharakan 1978). He acquired land in Koppa Kadoor in Chikamagalore in 1921-22, which was then in the Mysore State. However majority of them went to the Malabar district. Most of them also originated from the three mid-land taluks of Meenachil, Muvattupuzha and Thodupuzha. Though during the 1930-40 decade the flow picked up the peak flow occurred during the decade starting from 1940 and it is reported that in 1951 there were 70000 migrants in 50 settlements in Malabar (Tharakan 1978:295). Between 1950-60 and in the early 1960's apart from the outgrowth of earlier settlements new ones emerged. Though the flow continued in the later decades too the size of flow was subdued.

In the beginning there were two types of migrants-small and big farmers. In fact the pioneers were the big farmers who went out to extend their plantation in Malabar. They shuttled between Malabar and Travancore leaving the supervisors in charge of the farms. As against this the small farmers went for permanent settlement. As coastal region of Malabar was then densely populated it was in the hilly tracts that most of them settled, as cultivable land was cheaply available. Also the climatic condition was suitable for cash crops in which they were interested. The northern taluks were so attractive and even here Wayanad was so important the migration to Malabar was considered as Wayanad migration.

Indications are also that the first migrant to Wayanad originated from the Meenachil taluk of Pala. They settled at the place called Payyampally near Manantavady town. The town was then accessible by road from Thalassery. Following this the flow continued through out the length and breadth of the Wayanad district. Though the settlement of Travancore people in Wayanad started emerging from 1920's migration to Pulpally was a later development. It was only by the close of the 1940's that knowledge about this little world known outside. On going through some of the scattered pieces of evidences as well as based on our detailed field level discussions we are to conclude that the first migration of Travancoreans to Pulpally took place in 1948 and the first migrant was Panachikal Matthai. Before coming to Pulpally he lived in several other places in Malabar and it was finally from Payyampilly (where the first migrant settlement emerged in Wayanad) that he shifted to Pulpally. At Payyampilly he was engaged in petty trading and farming. The idea of migrating to Pulpally struck his mind very casually. To state, for the annual celebrations of the Sita Devi temple at Pulpally people from different parts of the region used to gather. It was also the only occasion when all the goods are made available at Pulpally as a market (locally known as chanda) used to be organised. Traders from neighbouring towns of Sultan Battery, Manantavady and from the neighbouring states of Karnataka and Tamil Nadu used to set up stalls. Mathai used to come for the celebrations. An idea of setting up a teashop struck in the mind of Mathai in 1947. Thus on 4th January 1948 on the first day of the annual festival itself he set up a teashop along with his son George. He made substantial earnings and a liking for Pulpally developed in his mind. While returning home Matthai discussed with his son the idea of settling at Pulpally. He agreed. On reaching home the matter was further discussed with his wife Annamma and she too agreed. Most of the lands in Pulpally at the time were held by the Pulpally devaswom. As per the prevalent regulation i.e. the Malabar Private Forest Act forestland can be given for cultivation on rent (charthikotukkal) only with the permission of the District Collector. It was also the time the devaswom manager applied for a sanction to offer 2000 acres of land for cultivation on lease. The passion of settling in Pulpally developed day by day in Matthai's mind and efforts were also underway. He was not prepared to wait till the Collector's permission. In Marakavu, in a place known as Palayanmoola situated just on the banks of Kadamanthodu River he bought a piece of land from the then Village Officer. On the other side of the stream was the land of Devaswom. On the purchased land he constructed a hut and the family of Matthai shifted from Payyampilly. Thus came the first Travancore migrant to Pulpally. He started selling the essential household goods on head load at the doorsteps of the households. In return apart from cash he collected the tradable goods from the households. Thus he became the first trader of the area. The job made him fully conversant with the geography of Pulpally and its people better than any others including the devaswom staff. In course of time Matthai developed contact with the devaswom manager. By the time permission for the lease of land was granted by the Collector to the Pulpally devaswom. It was also advertised that the Pulpally temple land would be given on Marupattam charthu on Rs. 5 per acre as manusham. Though the advertised rate was Rs. 5 the actual rate was Rs. 40 out of which Rs. 5 belonged to the temple and the balance amount was appropriated by the manager. Thus by 1950 started the flow of people to Pulpally for settlement. While some shifted from other settlements others were fresh migrants from the Travancore area. Matthai acted as an agent for many land deals, as he was able to arrange the type of land in accordance with the financial status of the migrants being familiar with the landscape of the area. It was also heard that a situation developed that only through Matthai the land deal can be made.

In the initial years there was only peripheral growth in settlements. However by the middle of 1960's the momentum gained and there was an unprecedented increase in the flow of migrants. In the annals of the history of this migration Pulpally migration will be remembered as an important event. There are reasons to this. Vast area was uninhabited and was thick forest. Most of the land also belonged to the Pulpally devaswom. The management was corrupt and inefficient. Even some of the land deals were executed orally and as stated by some of them, the devaswom authorities allotted the same land a second time. Even though guards were appointed it was impossible to guard properly the extent of land property owned. There was no demarcation of the transacted land. Even the devaswom security guards admitted settlers by accepting money. The status of the land thus came to be treated as one of common property resource giving room for large-scale encroachment. Thus individually and in-groups the land of their liking was grabbed. For all practical purposes the move can be said as organised. They aided mutually in establishing the right on the land. While one category took the land on charthu from the devaswom some others in addition to the contracted land extended their boundary. Also there was a significant number who purely encroached the land and settled in gross violation of all the laws. The usual practice was to establish one's claims over the land by carving certain alphabets (usually their name) on all the boundary side trees. On such demarcated plots usually as a matter of mutual understanding between the migrants no one stake any claim though even on some demarcated land later encroachment took place. Some of them even sold the demarcated land as forest without any valid ownership rights. To cite a case one of our respondents encroached 70 acres of land out of which 40 acres were given to another migrant accepting some money. It is also interesting to note that a few who were staying in the neighbouring villages too had encroached the land and established their right. Some even brought people from native place, provided shelter and other helps to encroach the land. Their strategy was to develop a colony of their community if not relatives. Finally to state even the land owned by the Survodaya Sanghom for distribution to the landless was not spared.

Speculative land deal also occurred. Thus a few contracted land en block by paying an advance to the devaswom. It was hatched between the devaswom authorities and big timber merchants and other business people. The idea was to fell the trees and thereafter to give the land to the cultivators. However on such land too encroachment occurred. All this practices were also aided by the prevailing political situation in the state. In the second half of the sixties the Communist party was governing the state. They had a soft corner towards the migrants and in some of their pronouncements this was clearly evident. To note one of the Ministers is said to have stated that if one farmer is evicted nine farmers will encroach the land. No doubt within a short period vast area got inhabited by the migrants a significant number of them occupying the land illegally. First the encroachment occurred far from the temple surroundings to escape the immediate notice of the authorities and the temple guards. Later it was extended towards the temple, which was the main centre of Pulpally. No doubt this paved the way for protracted agitation and confrontation with the devaswom authorities. This also gave birth to the formation of a revolutionary organisation called Naxalbari. Their violent attacks made Pulpally notorious all over. On this we make a detailed note later. On the incidence and the size of encroachment a brief mention may be made now.

Land Transacted/encroached

As mentioned above the influx of population continued at an unabated scale during the 1950's and 1960's and the forests became inhabited by the migrants. A number of them were purely encroachers and possessed the land illegally. To get a reflection of this magnitude we collected data of land possessed by the households at the time of migration. The result revealed that 52 migrant households resorted to pure encroachment over an area of 462.34 acres on an average 8.89 acres per migrant. Another 38 resorted to both purchase and encroachment and the size of encroachment on their part on an average came to 12.67 acres per migrant (481.46 acres). Thus the 90 encroachers on an average encroached 10.48 acres (943.80 acres). The range was from 0.90 to 70 acres. The size distribution of land encroached is shown in Table 4.1. While more than one fifth of them encroached up to 2.5 acres an equal size encroached between 2.51 - 5 acres, 14.44 percent between 5.01 - 7.50 acres and 16.66 percent between 7.51 to 10 acres. More

Table 4.1

Distribution of land encroachers by size of land encroached

Size of land (acre)	Number	Percentage
Up to 2.50	19	21.11
2.51-5.00	19	21.11
5.01-7.50	13	14.44
7.51-10.00	15	16.66
10.01 and above	24	26.67
All	90	100.00

than one fourth of them grabbed above 10 acres. All this reveals that the size of land encroachment was substantial. As to the incidence out of 194 respondents 46.39 percent were illegal encroachers. The size distribution of land transacted is shown in Table 4.2. The land formally transacted by the 142 migrants came

Table 4.2

Distribution of migrants by size of land transaction

Land size (acre)	Number	Percentage
Up to 2.50	49	34.50
2.51-5.00	43	30.28
5.01-7.50	18	12.68
7.51-10	13	09.15
10+	19	13.38
All	142	100.00

to 1170.08 acres (on an average 8.24 acres per migrant). There was wide variation and the range was from 0.10 to 270 acres. To mention one of the migrants later surrendered 85 acres as surplus land when the land reform legislation was implemented in the state. It is observable that 64.78 percent of the migrants purchased less than 5 acres and another 21.83 percent between 5.01 to 10 acres. The balance 13.38 percent contracted above 10.01 acres. On an average it can be found that the size of land possessed by the migrants in the beginning was 10.90 acres. What is more revealing to note is that for every acre transacted 0.81 acre was encroached by the migrants.

Land encroachment had a religious dimension. Table 4.3 is revealing the same. Out of 943.8 acres of land encroached 780 (82.64 percent) was encroached by the Christian community on an average 13 acres per migrant. In fact the data revealed the largest encroacher also as a Christian. This was followed by the Muslims as 9 persons on an average encroached 7.56 acres. The lowest was by 21 Hindus on an average 4.56 acres. In

Table 4.3

Religious distribution of land encroachers

Religion	No.of households	Area (acre)	Average area (acre)
Christians	60	780.00	13.00
Muslims	9	68.04	7.56
Hindus	21	95.76	4.56
All	90	943.80	10.48

terms of incidence the data makes interesting observation. The incidence was highest among the Muslims as 75 percent of Muslims encroached the land while the corresponding proportion was 46.51 percent among Christians and lowest 39.62 percent among the Hindus. In this background let us consider the characteristics of the migrants.

Place of Origin

The place of origin of the respondents is shown in Table 4.4. By and large most of them originated from the Southern Kerala as 74.23 percent of them reported Travancore as the place of their origin. While 18.55 percent belonged to the Northern Travancore and

Table 4.4

Place of origin of the migrants

Name of the region	Number	Percentage
Southern Travancore	144	74.23
Northern Travancore and Cochin	36	18.55
Malabar	14	7.22
All	194	100.00

Cochin region only 7.22 percent originated from the Malabar region.

Causes of Migration

What factors motivate people to move out is an important observation in migration studies. Explanation had gone beyond economic reasons as historical, geographical, sociological, institutional and political reasons are cited as influencing the migration decision. In the case of the present migration some of the reasons appears as true as apart from economic reasons a number of other factors were at work. On the economic front the developments in the Travancore region was such that there was wide spread poverty and misery. A number of factors contributed for this development. The region was characterised by commercialisation of agriculture in which plantation crops dominated. High population pressure exacerbated the situation as far as land availability is concerned. The social set up was quite feudalistic in nature with high land concentration. The tenants were squeezed as most of the products have to be given to the landlord as rent and their indebtedness was on the rise. Given the situation the thinking of some of them went on the line that wild animals will have much more concern for them than the landlords. Above all this there was food scarcity associated with the world war as the materials were diverted for the war purpose. Though public distribution system was set up it was peripheral in nature. To increase paddy production though reserve forest was given for agricultural purpose for three years the influential cornered them and cultivated the most profitable crops. All this meant more misery to the common man. Some other social problems were also hurting the common man badly. In the forefront was the dowry system, which was more deep rooted among poor Christian households. Some of the developments on the political front also tended the people to flee. Though the Travancore region was ruled by the King actually Sir. C P Ramaswamy Iyer ruled as a dictator. The common man was sharing more of the burden. For a more democratic set up Travancore State Congress was formed and agitation was going on. It was at its climax in 1930's. There was also suppression of the movements by force. Thus freedom of organisation came to be restricted. Further on the political front there was the emergence of the communist movement. Their preaching was to prepare for the revolution to overthrow the capitalistic order. There were uprisings too and the 1946 September 26 Punnapra Vayalar firing on communist workers was one such. Thus uncertainty too prevailed. In addition to all this the independence movement also generated a lot of heat on the political front as the King allied with the British. No doubt it was the poor who suffered on account of the misrule, revolt, class conflict, suppression etc. All this meant that the people have started thinking of going to Malabar on permanent settlement. In this context it may be mentioned that the Malabar Tenancy Act of 1930 ensured fixity of tenure to the cultivators on wet land, freedom from eviction from kanam lands and reduced fee payable at the time of the renewal of the kanam tenure. This strengthened the position of tenants. This too induced peasants to migrate.

In the course of our fieldwork we also made an attempt to elicit from the respondents the reasons for migration. The reasons cited were more or less the same as can be observed from Table 4.5. While 43.18 percent

Table 4.5
Reasons for migration

Reasons	Number	Percentage
Poverty	76	43.18
To have more land	60	34.09
No land	27	15.34
For economic betterment	6	3.41
Others	7	3.98
All	176	100.00

(Only 176 was able to state the reason)

cited poverty as the main reason, landlessness and urge to have more land were cited by 15.34 percent and 34.09 percent, respectively. Another 3.41 percent cited that for economic betterment they migrated. Other reasons cited run on the lines of marriage, casual visit, to join relation etc. It can be concluded that by and large it was the landlessness and poverty that drove many to Malabar.

Religion and Caste

A common perception was that the Travancore settlers in Malabar were the Christians. This is only partially true as a significant number from other communities too migrated to Malabar. However their settlements were concentrated as while in some areas the settlers are exclusively Christians in others it was somewhat religiously mixed. Still it is a fact that the Christians dominated in all the settlements. Pulpally is an exception to this as the settlers belonged to diverse religions and this is also one of the peculiar features of Pulpally compared to other settlements. The religious distribution of settlers is shown in Table 4.6. The table reveals that nearly two third of the migrants were Christians followed by Hindus 27.32 percent. The balance 6.19 percent was Muslims. It is revealing to note that though dominated by the Christians a significant number of them belonged to the Hindu religion. It will be interesting to observe the sub-division to which the Christians and Hindus belonged as the two communities have rigid sub divisions. The sub division of Christians by rites is shown in Table 4.7. Nearly three fourth of

Table 4.6

Religious distribution of migrants

Religion	Number	Percentage
Christians	129	66.49
Muslims	12	6.19
Hindus	53	27.32
Total	**194**	**100.00**

Table 4.7

Category wise distribution of Chiristian migrants

Category	Number	Percentage
Roman catholics	96	74.42
KCP	2	1.55
Jacobites	24	18.60
Protestants	5	3.88
Malankkara	2	1.55
Total	**129**	**100.00**

the Christian migrants were Roman Catholics. They were followed by Jacobites, 18.60 percent. Other denominations of KCP, Protestants and Malankkara Christians are considerably less in number. Now when considered the Hindus (Table 4.8) it can be observed that nearly three fourth of the Hindu migrants were Ezhavas (they belong to the other backward community) followed by forward caste Nairs 15.09 percent and other backward communities 7.54 percent. Those belonging to the SC/ST households were notably low, 3.77 percent. On the whole thus it can be observed that the migrants predominantly belonged to the Christian community and within the same community they were the Roman Catholics. Most of the Hindu migrants belonged to the Ezhava community.

Table 4.8

Caste wise distribution of Hindu migrants

Caste	Number	Percentage
Nairs	8	15.09
Ezhavas	39	73.58
Other backward communities	4	7.54
Scheduled castes	2	3.77
All	53	100.00

Year of Migration

Flow of people from Travancore region to the Malabar region started from the early 1920's. However as stated earlier Pulpally witnessed the flow at a later stage. This was on account of the fact that initial migration was close to the already existing human settlements where social and economic infrastructure facilities have developed at least peripherally. Viewed from this angle Pulpally was a very remote area and as per our observation the first migration occurred in 1948 and it continued till 1984. A few of our respondents belonged to the second generation of settlers and hence they were not able to state the year of migration. Still from the oldest person available within the household the information regarding the year of migration was ascertained and the result is shown in Table 4.9. It is revealing to note that nearly two fifth of the migrants

Table 4.9

Year of migration

Period	Number	Percentage
Before 1950	17	9.09
1951-57	36	19.25
1958-64	38	20.32
1965-71	73	39.04
1972-78	18	9.63
After 1979	5	2.67
All	187	100.00

came during the 1965-71 period. While 20.32 percent migrated during the 1958-64 period 19.25 percent migrated during the 1951-57 period. Thus the table reveals that migration which gained notable momentum in the middle of 1950's accelerated during the 1965-71 period. Thereafter the size of migration had slowed down and in the post 1979 period the size of migration worked out to 2.67 percent of the total. Thus it appears that most of the migration in Pulpally (78.61 percent) occurred during the two decades starting from 1951.

An attempt was also done to know the age and the generation to which our respondents belonged by ascertaining the respondent's relation with the first migrant of the family. The tabulated result shown in Table 4.10 reveals that 91 (46.90 percent) were the first generation in the sample and another 71(36.59 percent)

Table 4.10

Age at migration

Age group	Generation					
	First	Percentage	Second	Percentage	Third	Percentage
Up to 18	2	2.20	62	87.32	1	100.00
19-30	58	63.74	8	11.27	-	-
31-42	25	27.47	1	1.41	-	-
43-54	6	6.59	-	-	-	
55 and above	-	-	-	-	-	-
Total	**91**	**100.00**	**71**	**100.00**	**1**	**100.00**

were second generation. The age at migration is also shown in the same table. At the time of migration as can be observed from the table most of them were in their young age as 63.74 percent were in the 19-30 age group and another 27.47 percent belonged to the 31-42 age group. While two of them (2.20 percent) were in the up to 18 age group 6 (6.59 percent) were in the 43-54 age group. We have noted that none belonged to the above 55 age group. Evidently the migrants were either in the young or middle age group at the time of migration. The ventures they have undertaken were more hazardous and challenging. Uncertainty too loomed large as to the success of their mission. Thus it was the young and the middle aged who set out for the enterprise. It can also be observed from the table that those who belonged to the second generation of the migrants at the time of migration were in their teen age as 87.32 percent were aged less than 18 and another 11.27 percent in the 19-30 age group. Only 1 (1.41 percent) was in the 31- 42 age group. Among the third generation with the lone exception of one the age at the time of migration we were not able to ascertain and the one belonged to the up to 18 age group. Thus on the whole it can be seen that most of the settlers were in their prime age when they came to settle in Malabar.

Education

Education is an important indicator of the socio-economic status. To view the status of the migrants from this angle only the educational level of the first generation of migrants was considered. The same is shown in Table 4.11. By and large most of them were literate with formal schooling as 94.51 percent had

Table 4.11

Level of education of the migrants

Level of education	No. of migrants	Percentage
Illiterates	3	3.30
Literates but no schooling	2	2.19
Up to 4	39	42.86
5-7	20	21.98
8-10	24	26.37
11 and above	3	3.30
All	91	100.00

formal schooling. While 42.86 percent had schooling up to 4 years 21.98 percent had schooling between 5-7 years and another 26.37 percent between 8-10 years. The size of illiterate population was only 3.30 percent. Thus it emerges that the educational level of the settlers was on the higher side. This is not unexpected as Travancore-Cochin area was ahead of the Malabar region in the development of education. The majority also belonged to the Christian community which was educationally developed.

Land Ownership

The migrants were in search of cultivable land adequate in size at least to sustain the households. This naturally meant that most of them were land poor at the time of migration. To highlight this and also to get an overall reflection on the economic condition let us consider the size of land owned by the migrants at the place of origin at the time of migration. The size of land owned is shown in Table 4.12. Out of 173 persons we

Table 4.12

Size of land ownership of the migrants at the native place

Size of land (acres)	Number	Percentage
Up to 0.50	44	32.59
0.51- 1.00	26	19.26
1.01 - 2.00	35	25.93
2.01 - 3.00	13	9.63
3.01 and above	17	12.59
All	135	100.00

(Only 135 funished the data)

covered 135 were able to furnish the data of size of land owned per family at the time of migration in the native place. On an average the holdings worked out to 1.77 acres including the paddy field. The distribution by size of holdings shown in the table reveals that nearly one third had land holdings up to half an acre. While one fifth held between 0.51-1 acre another quarter owned between 1-2 acres. While 9.63 percent owned between 2-3 acres another 12.59 percent owned above 3.01 acres. Thus majority of them owned less than one acre. The data also revealed that nearly 19 persons were landless at the time of migration. Another interesting observation that can be made from the data is that ownership of paddy field was conspicuously low among the households. Out of 135 persons 17 reported ownership of paddy fields. All of them put together owned 14.45 acres giving an average ownership holding of 0.85 acre per family. The evidence indicates that the migrants were landpoor. One of the prominent reasons for migration was also search for cultivable paddy field, as the problem of availability of paddy field was much more serious among them.

Further evidence as to the economic status of the migrants can be had by looking at their perceived economic status. To get an overall profile on this issue we have asked the respondents to indicate what was their economic status before migration. The result again revealed that 167 (86.08 percent) stated that their economic status was low at the time of migration. While 24 (12.37 percent) stated their status as middle 3 (1.54 percent) households were in the upper strata. Thus it can be seen that most of the outflow from Travancore-Cochin state to Malabar occurred among the economically poor households. No surprise in view of their depressed state many conceived migration to Malabar as the solution. The depth of the sufferings they underwent in the course of the journey is further illustrative of their social and economic status then. A brief account of this will be interesting to note.

The Voyage to Malabar

Compared to other migration streams migration of Travancore peasants to Malabar had distinct features. The pitiable condition of living drove them away to Malabar. Migration was also permanent and hence they have to leave once for all the place of their origin to a very hazardous region. They knew nothing about the land and the people around. The relatives and friends on whom they looked upon for help and guidance and with whom they interacted daily as part of their social life since birth are to become a thing of the past. Institutions like church with which they have inseparable and close to heart relation is to become alien to them. These thoughts and stresses are at its climax the day before their departure. The scene and their actions were touching. Thus most of the relatives and friends assemble in the house of the migrant prior to the day of the departure. In the evening the migrant and his family go to the nearby Church to which they have a feeling of belonging and offer prayers. They know never again in their life they may not be able to offer prayers as one of the members of the Etavaka (the households covered by the Church). In the night except children no one sleeps and they engage in chatting. The topics centre on their miseries, about Malabar, the earlier migrants and their experiences, the hazards of Malabar life etc. Meanwhile the preparations are also done for the journey mainly bundling the bare requirements for their living at the new place. The bundles usually contain mats, available varieties of seeds, agricultural implements, clothes, utensils and to say whatever is manageable to them in their journey. In the morning a feeling of helplessness and tension pervade in the face of all. Hugging and a group weeping bids farewell to the migrant. A noted novelist commented the scene as " Matthai Adhomukhanayi (disappeared) followed by the children like dogs". Thus the journey commences. This was supposed to be the scene in most of the poor Christian households of Travancore during the early migration years. No doubt unable to cope up with the then prevailing situation it is said that several committed suicides. It was with full of anxiety and conflict in mind that they depart. The journey to Wayanad is another tale of misery. By the State transport bus or in a boat they reach either at the Alwaye or at the Cochin harbour station to catch the train up to Shornur. All of them vacate the train at the Shornur railway station being the boundary station between the Travancore-Cochin State and the Malabar district. As depicted by one of them the scene on the platform was equivalent to that of refugees as they have to spent hours guarding the bag and luggage with the accompanying wife and children for hours. At the station all the belongings are subjected to thorough checking before they are allowed to board the train to Malabar. In the process the treatment meted out by them were also inhuman as it is believed that they are deported by the King and their officials from the land for their criminal activities. Thus they were branded as thieves, dogs etc. and as recollected by them they were the moments when their self-respect was lost. In this context it also need to be mentioned that there were a few anti socials among them who were unable to continue in their native place. Thus in anxiety and fear they spent hours in the platform. When the train comes their feelings are at its climax as all the belongings and the accompanying females and children have to be pushed into the train. Cases of missing children and baggage were not an isolated event in the midst of the huge crowd. Anti socials also thrived by robbing their valuables and all these miseries gets burst in the train compartment in the form of loud cries. As plainly put by many in this situation the thinking of females was that even if died out of poverty it would have been better to remain at the native place. For a moment even the thinking of the males too went on the line as recalled by a number of them. Still the chance for a better morrow gave them the much-needed strength to march to the new land. Their train journey gets terminated either at Kozhikode or Thalassery. From there they have to catch bus and there are agents arranging the travel after an overnight stay at the hotel. Thus either they reach Panamaram from Kozhikode or from Thalassery taking another bus from Manantavady they reach Vairakuppa (a village of Mysore situated by the side of the Kabini river). The most dangerous course of the journey comes in the final phase and it is the journey through the thick forest on foot with head load of belongings for more than 10 kms. Finally they enters the Pulpally village.

Type of Migration

The flow of people occurred in several forms and in phases. Let us now make a note of this issue. Since the movement is for permanent settlement in an area, which is underdeveloped and exposed to all forms of natural calamities including attack of wild animals, sometimes the first to migrate are the males. They moved either singly or in-group. Family also moved either singly or in-group. The break up of migration by this categorisation shown in Table 4.13 reveals that 70.62 percent of the migration occurred with family and another 24.23 percent singly. While 3.61 percent migrated singly in-group the balance 1.55 percent migrated with family in-group. In view of the high incidence of single migration it will be interesting to know how soon the family was brought. The data

Table 4.13

Type of migration

Type	Number	Percentage
Single	47	24.23
Single in group	7	3.61
With family	137	70.62
Family in group	3	1.55
All	194	100.00

revealed that while the range was from 15 days to six years on an average it took one year and four months for the single migrants to bring their family in the new place of settlement. In this context it may be mentioned that a number of migrants were shifting from other settlements to Pulpally in their on going search for more fertile land and hospitable place. Also in some of the settlements they came across a variety of problems. Some of the problems were lack of proper title to the land, isolation and discrimination, problems in striking marriage alliance etc. A typical case may be cited. N K Gopalan belonging to the Hindu ezhava community at present aged 47 migrated from the Travancore region. First he migrated to Koothattukulam in the Cochin

State. From there he shifted to Thamarassery in the Kozhikode district. The next shifts were to Payyannur and Veliyambra located in Kannur district. Finally he came and settled in Pulpally. One of the reasons for his shift was to search for more fertile land. In some of the settlements there was no proper title to the land to the owner of the land and disputes led to eviction. Further there were social problems of caste based discrimination in which in the school pupils were grouped by caste and allowed to sit.

How Migration was Financed

Unlike many migration streams, which were in search of jobs and also tending to be temporary this is permanent migration where the migrants have to build everything from scratch. They have also to dwell in a very harsh environment. Thus for various purposes funds are required. Land has to be purchased or leased in and a living place needs to be set up. Land also has to be developed for cultivation and until the yield flow they have to be sustained. Since they were moving out permanently many mobilised the funds by way of asset disposal mainly landed property. Thus out of 194

Table 4.14

Sources of funds for migration

Source	Number	Amount Rs.	Percetage	Av. Amount Rs.
Land disposal	119	723435	91.78	6079.29
Borrowings	7	13708	1.74	1958.29
Assets sold	23	51002	6.47	2217.47
All	149	788145	100.00	5289.56

migrants 149 reported as shifted with funds. At the same time a few came across on the strength of their labour power. On an average it was found that the 149 persons mobilised Rs. 5289.56 and the range was from Rs. 50 to Rs 1 lakh. The funds were mobilised from various sources and by and large land disposal contributed 91.78 percent of the funds (Table 4.14). By disposing other assets they raised 6.47 percent and the balance 1.74 percent constituted the borrowings.

The Problems of the Migrants

As outlined above even though the village was inhabited for centuries the living conditions at the time of migration were very primitive as development was unheard of. An inter-related social and economic structure also prevailed with very little interaction with the outside world. Influx of a totally alien class took place in this situation. The migrants were also less exposed to the rigors of Wayanad life and hence the initial problems faced by them were many. In fact it was a life and death problem to most of them- an agnipareeksha as put by some of them. A brief reference to the problems they faced and the strategy they adopted to cope up with the situation is most appropriate here. We may now outline them one by one in some detail.

Agricultural Problems

While coming to Malabar most of the migrants had one main ambition in their mind- by own farming they must have enough paddy and tapioca to fill the belly. Hence the search was for fertile and cheap land. In this respect Pulpally was the most favourably placed and hence an unprecedented inflow took place with in a very short time period. By illegal means many also came to possess land quite beyond their expectation. This necessitated proper planning and development of agriculture. However hurdles were many. There was no ownership right over the land. Without land title cultivation of perennial crops was not a sound proposition. Even if there was ownership title to the land there are other problems. The nature of land was one formidable problem as it was thick forest. The growth of bamboo was so extensive that many even feared whether in their life time they could clear them and develop the land for farming. Also as per the prevalent regulations felling of trees on forestland was forbidden except Janmam lands. Above all there was scarcity of finance and their only capital was their own labour power. In this dilemma the initial plan went on the lines of developing a piece of plot at least to sustain them. Thus to start with male and female members of the households worked day in and day out and developed a small part of the land. To some extent the nature was also bountiful to them. Specifically in one of the initial years of migration bamboo flowering, which occur once in 20 years, happened. This led to the natural decay of the bamboo forests. Thus subsistence farming came to be practiced. On garden land paddy was grown known as Karuthan and hence they pioneered in introducing paddy cultivation on garden lands. The natives too followed the practice. Also it was the migrants who introduced the tapioca cultivation in the area as some of them brought the seed from their native place. In respect of the other crops the practices of the locals were adopted. As land for subsistence farming developed a stage came for the development of agriculture on commercial scale. Favourable conditions also emerged. The initial farming experiment was most successful and this gave them the much-needed confidence to undertake agriculture on commercial basis. Some marketable surplus a number of them were able to generate. Here again there surfaced problems. Vast areas can be developed only with hired labour. Among the migrants hardly any hired labour was available as most of them came for own cultivation. The source of labour supply in the village was the Tribes. Here again most of them were attached with the Chetty households more or less on permanent basis. Even if not attached labour availability to the migrants turned out to be a problem due to certain social problems. We shall make a specific reference to this shortly. Given such constraints a number of them practiced labour exchanges called Mattalpani in which the households pooled their labour and worked in the land of one at a time on rotation basis. In the system there was no wage payment. Only food was provided. In this context it may also be noted that there were a few who came with labour power to work and they were the only source of labour supply to the migrants in the beginning. Gradually to attract the tribal labour they evolved strategies. In this they succeeded.

Natural calamities and attack of wild animals to crops was another serious problem. High-speed wind was one of the threats to crops. They used to be protected by planting trees in the boundary. Attack of wild animals like elephants, pigs, monkeys etc was another problem. Regular guard was maintained by setting up erumatam on trees to create sound to drive away them. Also animals were frightened with crackers. Inspite of all this large-scale crop loss used to be suffered by most of them. Some of them reared dogs to drive away the monkeys. The strategy was ineffective as the tigers killed most of the dogs. No surprise some even abandoned their land and either settled in other safer places or returned home.

Marketing of agricultural products was another problem. The nearest market was 30 kms away and the products had to be transported on head load. Even to sharpen the work implements they have to go 13 kms away. In the course of time as marketable surplus resulted traders started coming to purchase the products. However they were subjected to intense exploitation. In the system an adequate price they were not able to realise. Also in weighing malpractice used to be done. To do this when the trader lands at the place in the morning message gets spread. The crops are then harvested. The traders come deliberately in the night to purchase the products. As all gathered together total confusion prevailed. Foul play in marketing was practiced in such a way that the Pandham (a lighting system in which cloth rolled on a stick is immersed in oil and set fire) was placed in their hand so that they are not able to correctly watch the weighing process. In the absence of other alternative marketing outlets they had to be contended with what was offered by the trader. Prices were also subjected to wild fluctuation. Small farmers were the most vulnerable. While at the time of harvest price get unduly depressed price go up later. As they have no means to stock the products they have to be contented with the low harvest time price.

Financial Problems

Absence of credit facilities was another problem faced by the migrants. Except a few Chetty households the rest of the households were leading a hand to mouth existence. Thus scope for borrowing was practically non-existent. The only source was the gold loan that can be availed from the Catholic Syrian Bank branch at Manantavady. In the beginning at sowing season most of them raised loans. It was again an ordeal and there was uncertainty too as to the availability. Thus in the morning one starts on foot with a food packet. By evening he reaches the town. The night has to be spent there. Some spent on the varandha of the shops. The other alternative was to avail a birth (a mat) in the restaurant for which Rs. 1 has to be paid. By morning at about 4 they have to be in the queue in front of the bank as people from various parts of the region gather for the purpose. As fixed amount is lent daily tokens are issued to those in the queue at the commencement of the business hours. One's luck gets tried there. If unlucky they stayed back and tried the next day. In dire need some of them even disposed the gold and mobilised the fund. In such a predicament some of them even disposed the wedding ring and the nature of their helplessness need no further comment.

Social and Religious Problems

The village which was uni-religious became multi religious on migration. The culture, life style, beliefs, customs and even the food habits of the migrants differed from the local inhabitants. While the locals were very conservative, lazy, inward looking and less exposed to modern value systems the migrants were more hard working, progressive and forward looking. The social problems the migrants face in such a set up can be said as all the more serious. Now let us take stock of the social and religious problems encountered by the migrants.

On the social front the migrants felt somewhat isolation from both the Tribal and the Chetty communities. Even the traders who visited the place looked upon them with contempt. This was invariably the experience of all the migrant communities as all of them were considered as Christians locally designated as Chettans. Even there was problem in getting labour supply to the migrants. The reasons were numerous. The migrants in general had a terrifying image among the locals. In the initial years there were some social problems of drinking and street fight among the few migrants. It is relevant to note here that a number of migrants flew from the native place unable to continue due to their anti-social activities. This they continued in the new place too. When they moved together in the night being not recognisable a deliberate attempt was made to create some kind of a terror image among the locals by shouting. At the same time in daytime they were very civilised. Needless to state this enabled some of them to grab land as natives hardly resisted. Christians were cow eaters. The locals considered buffaloes, as Demon and eating its flesh was something, which they cannot digest. Also rumour spread that they ate human flesh. An incident too strengthened this belief. In the village once at the burial place of a Chetty family an unearthed body of a Chetty was found in an eaten state. Though a wild pig did it the Christan migrants were accused of this. The news spread like wild fire. Also some migrants eat monkeys and this too reinforced such a belief. It was also spread that they have tails as in the dressing habit of females the tail of dhoti hang behind. Further the illegal activities of encroachment over the temple land have created a negative impression about the migrants among the locals. As a result of all this the local inhabitants in particular the Tribes in general looked up the migrants with fear. They hardly dared to come face to face. At the same time the migrants have been observed at a distance indirectly behind the trees. Cases do exist that some of the locals shifted out of the Christian settlement. Thus labour availability too turned out to be a problem for them. It cannot be denied that the Chetties had overblown these misgivings as they came to fear that their labour supply would dry up. No surprise gradually the migrants have been able to dispel these fears and succeeded in attracting the tribes. Strategies were evolved for the same. The tribes were offered paan, tapioca and other varieties of products. The items used to be exhibited and placed at a distance to enable them to pick up. Also those who were in good terms with the temple authorities persuaded the manager to allay the fears of locals to have interaction. To state some of them even entrusted cash with the Chetties for safe custody to build trust. Gradually the distance got narrowed and the Tribes started to mingle and offer labour to the migrants.

The migrants were untouchable to the Chetties even when they started interacting with them. Even the Tribes hesitated to take food from the migrant households since they were beef eaters. Chetties, when they offered eatables or drink to a migrant also offered water for cleaning the vessels and to keep it upside down as a mark of pollution. Migrants were also not admitted inside the house.

There were other problems quite serious in nature like getting matrimonial alliances. Here obvious discrimination existed even among the migrants. Those who were settled on plain lands in the lower ranges looked upon those settled in the high ranges as lesser ones. Even matrimonial alliances were not entertained as Wayanadans were considered as black and ugly. They were also considered as uneducated, uncultured and primitive.

The migrants were cut off from the family for considerable length of time. Even it was difficult to contact not to speak of frequent visits. The cultural and social life was one of pathetic. Even meeting people used to be a problem. As opined by a number of them the company of a neighbour was considered as equivalent to quenching thirst. For entertainment some used to gather by the side of the footpath and sing cinema songs. Flute music and beating on the empty tin bottles provided some rhythm for the songs.

Perhaps on the religious front came one of the worst forms of sufferings specifically for the Christians. Weekly prayers at Church on Sundays were considered as part and parcel of their life. There was no Church in the vicinity and the nearest Church was about 30 kms. away. Construction of Church in the temple land was also forbidden in the beginning. Once in a year they participated in the prayers at the Church. Later in a school shed at Mullonkolly, which was one of their earliest settlements within the village, they started gathering on Sundays for prayer. When order came for the lease of temple land a Church was set up in a shed and monthly the Vicar was brought from the neighbouring Church. Still on death and marriage occasions they came to notice the climax of their helplessness. Death occurs without receiving the last Kurbana (holy mass). The funeral procession was without any usual pomp and splendour- no accompaniment of golden/ silver cross, muthukuta, kuta bell, sorrow band and even the Priest and

Vedocharanam. All the migrants in the vicinity gather and that gave the colour to the function. An incident is further illustrative of their helplessness. When an old woman in the neighborhood died the settlers decided to give the final rest as per the Christian convention. Thus the body was laid in a bamboo box and carried by a group of persons for about 30 kms to the nearest Church. On reaching the Church the Vicar denied permission, as the last Kurbana was not received by the diseased. They were in a helpless state. Adventurism and courage develop in such a state. They threatened to leave without the body. Ultimately the Priest yielded and she was buried in the Church.

Food Shelter and Other Living Facilities

A brief note can also be made on the distress conditions of living. The houses were of the hut type, the features of which were mentioned in the earlier chapter. Clothing was inadequate. Due to severe cold conditions the nature of sufferings can only be left to one's stretch of imagination. Under severe cold lips and fingers used to bleed on getting dried. Even their practice of sleeping in front of the fire gave little relief. Some used to sleep with fire under the coat (coat made of bamboo). Houses were seldom secure from the attack of wild animals. Sometimes with family they used to sleep in the erumatam. On the sight of animals even pregnant women were led to the erumatam in the beginning. To mention one of our respondents lived on erumatam for three years. Several such cases were there.

On the food front the problem they encountered were much more serious. It was ration time and hence food grains movement was restricted. As narrated, one of them brought the paddy as seed from the native place inside the pillow with a mat covering. They used to smuggle in rice from Mysore through the forest. Drought years were much more vulnerable. Many recollected that in one such worst year if the nature were not bountiful many would have perished. In the year there was acute scarcity of food on account of the failure of monsoon. Nature however came to their rescue. There was a steep rise in the price of a herbal plant locally called Amalpori, which was then abundant in the Pulpally forests. It is said that there was not even a single migrant who had not gathered the plant sold and brought rice from the neighbouring Mysore State. Apart from scarcity of food there was lack of money. As we commented in the beginning even casual wage employment was not available. The cash they brought was used for some land transaction. Even if there was some balance it lasted for few weeks. Thus the initial period was marked by semi starvation and as stated by one for about one year the family lived on tapioca and rice soup. To illustrate the magnitude of sufferings in the beginning one of them instead of paying Rs. 1 to a tribal labour to transport the grinding stone the migrant brought it on head load through the forest for 13 kms. Further even if there was money goods were unavailable and they have to walk nearly 13 kms to the nearest market. Those who can afford used to stock for 3 to 6 months the essential goods. In this context it may be mentioned that to a certain extent invariably they too resorted to the practice of food gathering. Hunting and fishing was common. Also they collected several forest products and sold to earn money. Hence it can be said that the common property resources played an important role in sustaining the migrants in the initial years of migration. The local Chetties were also kept in good humour once contacts were established, as they were the only people on whom they can fall upon in times of acute distress. The Chetties were very generous. Thus they used to be approached for paddy, fruits like mango, jackfruit etc. Thus as acknowledged by most of them the Chetties too played a significant role in sustaining the migrants in the early years.

The migrants were even compelled to change the food habits. Rice was their staple food. Scarcity situation made it an occasional food. Tapioca became an important food item. Beef was one of the important item in the menu of Christians. In the initial years they had even foregone meat as killing cows was forbidden by the temple authorities.

Nature was bountiful as far as water is concerned. Water was clean and plenty. Even the stream water was fit for consumption. The ground water table was so favourable that a small pit used to provide water. The only problem was crabs, which used to stir water and make them muddy. Some of them used to fix hallow palm pieces as an outer cover to the pit to control the problem of crabs. As to the availability even some of them used to drink water from the pit formed out of the footsteps of wild elephants. At the same time to a number of the migrants due to locational disadvantages water was available at a distance. In such cases they used to channel the water through a channel made of bamboo. However the monkeys used to destroy them. Some also used to collect rainwater for household use.

There was a lot of uncertainty in travelling. Threat of wild animals was one factor. The other was climatic. A particular incidence is illustrative of their plight. On one rainy day one of our respondents went to dispose the product at Manantavady. On return the Kabini River was over flowing due to heavy rain and the country boat went upside down. He some how managed to get hold of a tree and spent the whole night on the tree. The next day the neighbours gathered for the rescue operation. A rope was offered and he was drawn the other side. All along, his family was crying from the other side of the river.

Threat to life also existed on the health front, as medical facilities were absent. Common diseases no body cared. Even if serious all remedies locally available was tried. Malabar was considered as synonymous with Malampani (Malaria). It was one of the dreaded diseases. The disease took a heavy toll of lives in the hilly regions of Malabar in the initial years. Skin disease, fever, jaundice and chicken pox were common. The nearest hospital was 30 kms away. Many died on the way including pregnant women. The sick were transported on chair by a group of 4 persons in times of emergency for hospitalisation and treatment.

To escape from severe cold they brewed liquor at home out of paddy called Nellu water (paddy water) in the beginning. This later got developed on a commercial basis. Associated with this also developed clashes and infighting among the migrants.

Apart from the attack of wild animals to standing crops they lived under perpetual fear from the attack of wild animals. Even the devaswom sent the elephants freely. The nights were noisy as to drive wild animals they used to make noise. Though cases are isolated some of them even left the land due to constant attack of elephants. The typical case was that of Baby who bought 5 acres for Rs.500. As he had to live under perpetual fear he discarded the land and moved to a much safer place. There he started working as agricultural labour. He now owns 12 cents of land and the old land was encroached by some of the later migrants. He is now even unable to locate the land.

The migrants were well aware of the benefits of education and were keen in educating the children. However educational problems were insurmountable in nature. At the time of migration there were only two lower primary schools one at Chekady and the other at Pulpally. To reach the nearest school the children has to traverse kms through the thick forest. Most of them were not prepared to undertake the risk and hence many were compeled to give up education in the beginning. Even if enroled it was done late and they were sent in groups. The strategy of others was to seek the help of relatives living in other places and hence children were sent at the relative's place for education.

As to the communication and transport the less said the better. Even news about death and other news reached weeks later making it impossible to attend to the cases in time. There was no transport facility. From Manantavady there was one direct bus to Kozhikode. Advance notice has to be given for the travel.

In the beginning language too was a problem as Chetties spoke a language of their own.

Other services also remained as problems. To mention even barbers were unavailable and as said without hair cut they were unrecognisable and looked like jungle man. Sometimes they mutually helped.

Attack of Gastroenteritis

As mentioned above health facilities were utterly lacking and hence they were prone to hazards of diseases. One of the worst suffering which still lingers in the mind of the Pulpally people was the attack of gastro. In 1971 April occurred the incident and the victims were the children. Death came within hours of the appearance of the symptom. Though there was one allopathic, homeopathic and ayurveda doctor each in Pulpally then, the facilities to treat large number of victims were absent. Unable to cope up with the situation the children were taken to the Vijaya High School and laid there so as to share the sorrow in-group. The consciousness of the people also got stirred. Frantic efforts were made to avert more tragedies. Though the District Medical Officer (DMO) located about 100 kms. away was informed over phone no succour came. In fact the response was indifferent and to state what they said was that the children of naxalites are dyeing, let then die (naxal incident we illustrate later). A group went and met the District Collector. The Collector directed the DMO over phone to attend to the case and it was agreed to visit the place and make a report. The DMO visited Meenangadi (30 kms away) and reported back that the problem was not serious. This version was reported in the daily newspaper. This agitated the people and a group of 12 persons went to meet the DMO to seek an explanation. It was almost midnight when they reached his house. In the meanwhile they informed the local M L A and the press about their plan. They in turn is said to have informed the police. By the time the group reached the DMO's house a police party also came. A few in the group reacted overly and started scolding the DMO and insisted that in the same state (dressed with a dhoti and banian) he should come out and make the necessary arrangements. Hearing the incident the police too had a soft corner towards them. Ultimately in the same state the DMO went to the Assistant Medical

Officer's house and arranged to send a vehicle with medicines and two doctors. By morning they reached Pulpally and the situation was brought under control. The DMO also visited Pulpally the same day. By evening a batch of 12 doctors with medicines were rushed to Pulpally by the Kozhikode Medical College. The incident however had ill effects. When a government hospital was soon started at Pulpally none of the doctors was prepared to come to Pulapally due to fear. Here again the local leaders struggled. They identified a willing doctor and got him transferred to Pulpally. This incident indicates that in times of crisis the people have acted collectively and there were persons to lead them.

Forced Eviction from the Land

Travancore migrants suffered a lot in the Malabar settlements in the initial years of migration on various counts. The nature of sufferings was illustrated above. While some of them were man made others were natural. This was true wherever they went and the difference was only in the degree of sufferings. The sufferings of Pulpally migrants were much more severe on all these counts. Over and above what was stated above and perhaps the worst form of their suffering was the forced eviction from the settlements. In fact it was a creation of their own.

As noted above in violation of all norms of civilised society the migrants occupied the devaswom land and started developing the land for agriculture. Though the devaswom authorities attempted to guard the property, unmindful of the same the illegal settlement continued. This also led to the forced eviction by way of removing or setting fire to the huts, removing all the belongings including work implements and destruction of standing crops. At one time special squads were appointed by the devaswom for the eviction of the cultivators. However the cultivators started occupying the same land. They also worked in union that within hours the evicted were resettled on the same land. To state one of the respondents was evicted 16 times from the land and still he continued to occupy the same land. The issue also became a serious law and order problem of the village. Thus at the request of the temple authorities an MSP (Malabar Special Police) camp was set up with 25 police personnel and two sub-inspectors. They were accommodated at the temple premise adjacent to the temple. They also let loose eviction proceedings. On the other side the organisation of the migrants also got strengthened day by day. Irrespective of the religion/ caste consideration the migrants resisted and they started projecting it as a human problem. The migrants have made deep inroads in several parts of Malabar. An organisation known as the Malanadu Karshaka Sangom too was formed as in most of the settlements in Malabar there were problems though not identical. It was to fight for their cause the Sangom was formed. In Pulpally also a branch was established as early as 1962.The organisation succeeded in developing considerable political influence and in turn the political parties held a soft corner towards them in consideration of their numerical strength and unity. In the forefront was the Communist party, which took it as a problem of the working class, no matter what their actions were. In fact it has been pointed out to us that the size of encroachment was at its peak during the Communist rule. In the middle of 1960's it was said that there were about 4500 families settled in Davaswom land. Only a fraction of them had made the land deal with the Devaswom. An objective look into the case will reveal that there were serious lapses on both sides. Some of the transactions were executed orally and there was widespread corruption in the deal. There was no proper demarcation of the land leased out. To say there was total mismanagement of the property on the part of the devaswom. The action of the migrants was much more illegal and contemptible. Still they resisted the forced eviction. It is significant to note that the Christian Church gave the leadership openly in their fight against eviction. At one stage the Pulpally Karshaka Sangom got neatly organised. The whole area was divided into seven wards and in each ward 7 units were constituted. Each unit had a Captain, a Secretary and seven Volunteers to protect the migrants of the unit. The eviction proceedings became a daily affair and the atmosphere also became charged full of tension. By the time the issue got wide publicity. At one point at the instance of the Church the Priest convened a meeting. Thus notices were issued to all households and an assembly of people was held to find a solution to the problem. The temple authorities were threatened to face the consequences unless the guards are withdrawn. Though the devaswom manager convened a meeting and discussed the issue no compromise was reached. In the meanwhile several representations were made by the migrants to the State government to redress their sufferings. The response was lukewarm. The eviction proceedings got intensified and the migrants started resisting them. July 1967 happened to be the final day. Eviction on massive scale was planned and started executing from one side of the village. The news spread all over. The Church bell rang to alert the people. All of them assembled in the Church. Immediate action was chalked out under the leadership of the Priest of the Church. Thus in procession they moved to resist the eviction under the leadership of the Priest. The school students were kept in front of the procession. The slogan that hit the already surged atmosphere was that even on firing they will not retreat and eviction can be done by killing them. A delegation was also then at the State capital seeking government action. Though initially they met a number of ministers no relief was in sight. Finally they met the Forest Minister who gave a patient hearing to their plight. Though he too expressed his helplessness, as it was encroachment over forestland it was agreed to stop eviction temporarily. Message was sent immediately to Pulpally through the District Collector. Quite unexpectedly the message came in the surged atmosphere and thereupon both parties disbursed. They never thought that their sufferings came to an end then. In fact it happened so. The temple authorities suspended the eviction of settlers. Later the Private Forest (Vesting and Assignment) Act was passed by the State Assembly to nationalise the private forests. Thereafter property rights were conferred to the possessors of land as per the Kerala Land Reforms Act. Thus in 1975 occupants were assigned ownership titles by the competent authority. The size distribution of the land distributed is shown in Table 4.15. The table reveals that 4837 persons were assigned land owned by the Pulpally devaswom. Nearly three fifth (59.29 percent of the beneficiaries) were Christians and 36.80 percent were non-tribal Hindus. The tribes constituted only 3.16 percent and the balance 0.75 percent were Muslims. In this context it may also be mentioned that most of them lacked the land tax receipt for the stipulated period to establish their claim over the land. Still all of them managed to establish the claim and how it was managed is a mystery. Quite interestingly a number of forged title deeds were also noticed as in circulation and it was

Table 4.15

Distribution of the beneficiaries by size of land assigned

Size of land (Cents)	Number	Percentage
Below 10	242	5.00
11- 25	330	6.82
26- 50	513	10.61
51- 100	879	18.17
101-150	612	12.65
151-200	520	10.75
201-250	369	7.63
251-5.00	864	17.86
501- 750	309	6.39
751- 1000	124	2.56
1001- 1500	70	1.45
1501- 2000	5	0.10
All	4837	100.00

Source: Mohandas M 1992:27.

known as Kuttappan Pattayam (Pattayam is the local name of the title deed and the brain behind the forged document was said as Kuttappan). It was said that they were indistinguishable from the one issued by the revenue authorities. There ends the long drawn drama played by the migrants. In the end the temple lost most of the lands. Though several cases were fought in the Court it was said that the temple authorities did not seriously follow up the cases. Thus out of the total land owned to the extent of 20000 acres today the Pulpally devaswom owns 34 acres of land. The apprehension is that even this land extent may fall short of 34 acres if it is measured now.

REFERENCES

Mohandas (1992), Op. cit.

Tharakan Michael (1978), Op.cit.

Chapter 5

Developmental Impact of Migration

"You may go the way I guide you leaving your place, your relations and your parental home. I will bless you; make you and your name very admirable and your people famous. Thus you become blessed," said the Lord to Abraham. Though this may be a mythical statement, in the case of the Pulpally migrants this turned out to be a reality as epic has been created out of adversities. Development of the village was unparalleled and the village carved out a niche of its own in the whole development map of the Wayanad district. Catalysts to this were the migrants. Now an excursion into the present social and economic structure of the village against the backdrop of the pre-migration conditions of the village and the people depicted in the earlier two chapters will amply bring out this fact. This will also provide an overall insight into the impact of migration.

Population and the Settlement Pattern

As per the 1991 census there was 30035 persons in Pulpally panchayat covering an area of 77.78 sq. kms. This gives a density of 386 persons per sq. km. This is higher than the density of Wayanad district, which was 315 in 1991. Thus the sparsely populated Pulpally became thickly populated. Also from a uni-religious population composition the change was to a multi religious population composition. The population consists of the Christians, Hindus and Muslims. Among the Hindus and Christians most of the denominations are found in the village. Also in size the alien population has overtaken the native population. All this stands out as unique features of Pulpally compared to any other settlement of the Travancore people in Malabar.

Though the population settlement is somewhat mixed by religion there are few pockets where people belonging to the three religions concentrate. The tribal population at the same time is colonised and there were 71 tribal colonies in the village.

The Pulpally Town

An outstanding development in the post migration period was the growth of the Pulpally town. What is more important to note is that the town has grown as one of the important towns in the whole of the Wayanad district. To state, before migration the important town centres in Wayanad district were Kalpatta, Manatavady and Sultan Battery. All of them were trading centres even before the migration. While Kalpetta is the district headquarter the other two towns are the taluk head quarters. Apart from being the taluk/district headquarters the locational advantage too contributed for the growth of these centres. Thus while Kalpatta and Sultan Battery lie on the Kozhikode-Mysore main road route Manantavady was situated on the Kalpetta-Kannur main road route. Where as Pulpally was remotely placed from the main road routes of Wayanad. Still in the course of our extensive visits to some of these towns of the district notably we learnt that Pulpally emerged as the fourth largest town in the district now. What is more significant to note is the fact that the Panamaram and Meenangadi were the two important trading centres even in the pre-migration era. In fact the people of Pulpally initially depended up on the Panamaram market for most of their requirements. Also Pulpally people used to go to Meenangadi market to dispose their agricultural products then. While Panamaram lie on the Kalpatta- Manatavady main land route Menangadi was located on the main land route of Kalpetta- Mysore. Still Pulpally town has overtaken the Panamaram and Meenangadi towns in size and in terms of the development of trade, transport, banking, social and economic infrastructure and other institutions. Here it is relevant to mention that many of the villages in Wayanad witnessed migration of people much earlier to the flow of migrants to Pulpally. None of these village centres have been able to register the type of development made by Pulpally.

At the side of the Sita Devi temple is situated the Pulpally town. In the centre of the town is the bus stand. A number of trading houses, hospitals, lodges, eating houses including bar hotels, schools, cinema houses etc. are located within the town. The town is well connected with most of the settlements by bus and jeep services. So also the Pulpally town is connected directly to most of the town centres of Wayanad as well as the neighbouring district headquarters of Kozhikkod and Kannur districts. Notably now a direct daily bus service covering about 350 kms. connects Pulpally to Pala, which is an important town close to the place of origin of the migrants. People more or less visit daily Pulpally town for shopping and for other purposes. A number of them also commute daily to the neighbouring towns and similarly a number of people from the neighbouring areas visit the town for various purposes. All this indicates not only that the isolation of the village has ended but also that there is a very mature level of interaction with the outside world.

Development of Infrastructure Facilities

As stated above transport and communication facilities were practically non- existent and the people traversed kms through thick forests just for purchasing their essential requirements. Though gradual the level of infrastructure development of all type registered by the village was commendable. Development of the transport facility was one of the most visible one. To begin with, by 1954 with the onset of migration a peripheral road was developed to connect Pulpally with Sultan Battery and a bullock cart started operating in the route as recollected by some of them. It was fully developed in 1971 and extended to Perikallur, which lie on the banks of the Kabini River. Thus people can cross the river in country boat and reach the neighbouring village of Karnataka. In the same year the first bus service started operating from Pulpally to Sultan Battery. Followed by this came the Pulpally- Naikuppa, Pulpally- Panamaram, Pulpally-Pakkam Dasanakkara, Pulpally- Kanichira roads connecting the town and the village with all the important neighboring towns and settlements. A network of roads were constructed within the village at the initiative of the migrants right from the beginning. The leadership came from the Church. Thus in each area the migrants in the forefront evolved the local road development plans and executed the works on all Sundays by pooling their materials and labour. On such days food was served in common. For the same as recollected by some of them buffalo used to be butchered on the spot and the beef curry was an attraction. Though depending on the availability of resources in some areas tribal labour was also employed by and large most of the road development in the village was the result of voluntary action of the people. Thus it can be stated that the village can claim the distinction of having executed the largest road development out of people's participation. No doubt resistance too was there from some quarters. Still on collective persuasion and at times by force they executed the road plans. To mention the strategy in one of the settlements, which was earlier part of Pulpally village, resistance came from one of the coffee estate owner. The plan was to give road connection to a small settlement by a link road. The estate had already a road link and hence the new road was found as redundant. Though the owner was persuaded several times he had not fallen in line. Ultimately by way of planned collective action the road was developed overnight. Thus over the years vast network of roads developed within the village. Though kucha road development in the settlement at the initiative of the community occurred on a grandiose scale pucca road development suffered. The settlers also came to recognise that there are limitations to their own voluntary actions and that without governmental initiative pucca road development was impossible. The ultimate solution they conceived was to send one of the persons from the area to the State legislature to claim at least their rightful share. By this time the people of the area particularly the migrants developed good political connections. Also for common purposes there was unfailing unity among the people. They succeeded in striking the deal and in 1970 Sri K Raghavan Master, a tribal person, was fielded from the South Wayanad constituency in the assembly election. He won the election and his party also came to power. The road and other infrastructure development got a big boost. Thus developed some of the pucca roads we have listed above. The later years witnessed profound growth of infrastructure in Pulpally. Thus today in terms of road development the village became most developed. To cite some road statistics, in the Pulpally Panchayat covering an area of 77.78 sq. kms there are now 252.9 kms. of roads and this gives 3.25 kms. of roads per sq. km. Out of the total roads 154.3 kms of roads (61.01 percent) were either tarred, metalled or soled roads. At the same time in the Wayanad district the total road length in 1998 was 679.2 kms (State Planning Board 1998: S 147). This gives a road length of 0.33 km. of roads per sq. km (0.57 km. road per sq. km at the State level). As to the road development of the village no further proof is required. Apart from the road route the village is also connected with the neighbouring Karnataka village by water route.

As far as the communication development is concerned the first telephone connection came up in the area in 1977. Subsequent to this came a telephone exchange at Pulpally and today there are over 1200 telephone connections within the Pulpally village giving 1 telephone connection per 22 persons. As against this at the district level the telephone ownership was 1 per 50 persons in 1998 (State Planning Board 1998: S 178). In addition it was noted that about 2000 applications for telephone connection are pending in the village. Coming to the development of postal service there are now 16 branch post offices and one main post office within the village. Thus there was one post office per 1518 persons in Pulpally while it was 1 post office per

5760 persons in the State in 1998 (State Planning Board 1998: S 107). The dimensions of developments on this front need no further comment.

Banking development is another notable feature. Now there are 4 branches of scheduled commercial banks functioning in the village. This gives 1 bank branch per 6453 persons in the village. At the same time at the district level the availability was only 1 bank branch per 10500 persons in 1993 (10086 State). Apart from this there are 2 co-operative banks and 8 private financiers in the village.

Social Infrastructure

Coming to the development of social infrastructure facilities of schools and hospitals it can be said that the achievements were quite praise worthy. As outlined earlier there were peripheral facilities for education and even the available facilities were inaccessible to most of them. With migration the scenario underwent changes. The migrants were very keen to impart education to their children as they firmly held the view that children's destiny should be different form their's. Hence all efforts were made to get them educated. Thus in the beginning they pooled money and materials to set up informal schools. Later most of them were raised to the status of formal school. Thus to trace the history around 1950 a few who settled in Veliyambam and Mullankolly set up an L P school and by 1954 in most of the settlements facilities for primary school education developed. In 1956 one of the schools in Pulpally namely the Vijaya Elementary School was upgraded to the status of an Upper Primary School. Up to 1964 this status continued and in the same year the school was again upgraded as a High School. Thus by 1964 the facility for high school education too got established in the village. To state the difficulty they encountered, to construct the school shed on head load for about 8 kms. the students and teachers transported the construction materials. Though the first high school came up in 1964 it was not recognised as an examination centre. Thus the first batch of 32 students and the teachers marched the day before the commencement of the examination behind an animal cart with their bag and baggage in the animal cart. All of them camped in the school till the completion of the examination. This continued till 1969 and in the same year the Vijaya School was recognised as an examination centre. To cite how fast was the development of the village on the educational front, in 1944 for the whole Wayanad area came the first high school at Kalpetta. In 1949 came another one at Manantavady. Thus before 1950 there was only two high schools in the region. After the formation of the State in 1956 came another high school at Panamaram followed by one each at Mepady, Sultan Battery, Nadavayal, Palllikkunnu and Pulpally in order. Thus the Pulpally high school was the eighth school started in the series. In sports and other fields the Vijaya School made notable contribution. In 1984 it was recognised as the best school in the district. The later decades too witnessed further leap forward in educational development of the village. By now there are 3 high schools, 5 U P and 9 L P schools functioning in the village. For higher education a college too was established in the village. It was the fourth college to come up in the Wayanad district. To illustrate the level of educational development the size of population per school/college in the village and the district is shown in Table 5.1. As can be discerned from the table the village is far ahead in the development of educational facilities compared to other areas of the district.

Table 5.1

Indicators of school development

Level of the schools	Wayand No	Population per school	Pulpally No	Population per school
Lower primary	127	5291	9	2868
Upper primary	77	8727	5	5162
High schools	61	11016	3	8604
Colleges	6	112000	1	25812

Coming to the availability of hospital facilities in the village there is one government hospital now with 26 beds, a public health centre and four 4 private hospitals. All this put together gives on an average 1 bed per 177 persons. If we consider only the hospital beds in the public hospital the availability was 1 bed per 993 persons against an availability of 1 bed per 829 persons in the district in 1998 (State Planning Board 1998: S250). In the public hospital works to add 20 more hospital beds are in an advanced stage of completion.

On the cultural front also there was notable development. There are roughly 75 social, literary and cultural organisations in Pulpally. For entertainments there are 5 theatres. In addition to this there are units of NGO's, YMCA, Sreyas, St Mary's and Junior Chamber in the village.

A number of government institutions catering to a group of villages are located in the village. To mention a Police Station with the status of a Circle office, Registration Office, Sub-treasury, Tribal Development Office etc. are some of them.

The Village Economy-Dynamics of Development

Nature and size of productive activity is an important determinant of the level of development of the village economy. On this front the economy is still rural as agriculture and allied activities constitutes the main economic activity. At the same time if diversification of the crop enterprises and intensive farming are reflective of the level of agricultural development, undisputedly the economy of the village has made tremendous development. Precisely the subsistence agriculture of the village has well responded to the new profitable opportunities with migration and the impact was all pervading. This may be spelt out in some detail.

Commercialisation of Agriculture

In the agricultural sector one of the significant developments was the commercialisation of agriculture. Commercialisation is a social process, which brings into focus relationship between producers on the one hand and agents engaged in input output markets, labour, credit and other agencies on the other. Thus what takes place is an integration of the village traders/ wholesalers into commercial structure and the agrarian economy develops strong backward and forward linkages. This is brought about through different methods. It may be a normal mechanism driven by market incentives or by involuntary process like indebtedness, state coercion, involuntary migration etc. Forced commercialisation has been linked with interlocked product, credit and labour markets. In this situation economic agents (money lenders, agents, landlords etc) exploit through dual channels. The normal process is associated with larger production gains as well as its just distribution. Both normal and forced commercialisation proceeds unevenly across regions and over time. In a normal process the size of marketable surplus depends on prices, level of output, size of holding, home requirement and cash needs of households. In the village the process was a natural outcome as there was the convergence of a number of favourable factors. It was also a migration-associated development as can be seen from the ensuing paragraphs.

While migrating most of them had only one main motivation and that was to make a reasonable living out of self- farming. When viewed from this perspective many of the migrants came to possess land beyond their expectation and the land was very fertile too. Given the resources such as capital and labour as also the other constraints we outlined above in the initial years only a part of the land they were able to develop. Hence the subsistence farming continued for some more time even after migration. At the same time they came to recognise the need to develop all the land and to practice commercial farming. Compulsion and an enabling environment too developed. There was no permanent title to the land. At the same time keeping the land as forest invite the risk of losing the land. This dictated the need to develop the land. The size of yield on the already cultivated land aided the process in two ways. On the one hand the high yield led to marketable surplus and hence surplus income formed the capital for land development. Also this gave them the much-needed enthusiasm to extend cultivation. In fact the expectations of the migrants aroused. No surprise a bigger agenda- farming above sustenance developed in them. Thus gradually production for sale has come to be practised and this led to the development of trade contacts and the development of market for agricultural products in the village. Thus the course of development that followed was the move from subsistence farming to a highly commercialised agriculture where commercial crops have come to claim most of the cultivated area. This process may be put in historical perspective in brief.

The process was gradual as our data reveals. On an average it took 4 years and seven months for the farmers to develop the land fully. The land was also developed in stretches. What they did was profitable level of crop diversification given some of the constraints we outlined in an earlier chapter. In this course of development the one crop enterprise, which found favour in the beginning, was lemongrass cultivation and oil distillation. This amply brought to the fore the enterprising character of the people as in the prevailing situation this turned out to be the most profitable venture. For distilling the oil as clearing of the forests for cultivation was going on firewood was available in plenty. The climatic condition demanded their exposure to heat. Liquor was an indispensable item to them given the severe cold condition and their daily hard physical work. The distillery too facilitated brewing of arrack. The crop was popularised by one Kurusingal Chakko who brought the seeds from the Central Kerala. He also functioned as an agent and advanced seeds, materials and money on the condition to sell back the oil. Advances were recovered in instalments. Thus most of the migrant households by pooling their own labour and employing marginal hired labour started producing the oil. The Chetties also followed their footsteps. When the activity spread people started marketing on their own either at Manatavady or Kozhikode. The cultivation laid the foundation for the economic prosperity of the farmers. On the one hand yield was high and on the other hand the price was very remunerative. It was indicated that in 1955 a bottle containing 650 ml of oil fetched Rs. 400 in the nearest market. The prosperity enabled them to make sizable investment in land and spread of consumerism. Overall diversification of demand led to the development of market for goods and all-round development. Side by side tapioca cultivation also developed on commercial scale. The soil fertility was so rich that without the application of any fertilisers they were able to make substantial yield. People said that for their consumption rather than plucking one plant they used to scratch the root and cut the requisite quantity, as the yield from a single plant was sufficient for many days. If entirely drawn from one plant the balance used to be kept in the soil. It is also said that when there was food scarcity in Kerala, Wayanad people made available tapioca and hence alleviated the poverty conditions to some extent. The fortune out of lemongrass cultivation however did not last long and several factors led to the extinction of lemongrass cultivation and oil production. First came the governmental regulations. Distillation was licensed. Also the oil has to be sold to the State Trading Corporation depot for which an attested certificate indicating the size of land cultivated was to be obtained from the Village Officer. Thus the right to sale was to those who possessed licensed distillery and sales can be done once in a month. There were also other hurdles. There was a check post on the way to the market. Normally sales tax has to be paid. Most of them evaded the tax. Thus they used to exit from the bus with the product and cross the check post point on foot through the forest speedily and again catch the same bus. At the depot again they are open to exploitation. The quality is examined in terms of the citrol content and minimum has to be satisfied. Many fail to satisfy the minimum stipulated citrol content due to the foul play of the dealer. Thus they are forced to sell the oil at a very low price to an unauthorised private agent operating the next door. The arrangement was evolved tacitly by the Depot Manager and the private agent. Above all this by the early 1960's there was a steep fall in the price of the oil. By the time the labour cost shooted up. Further firewood scarcity too developed and all this meant that lemongrass cultivation has to be given up once for all. From short duration crops the next shift was to the plantation crop and that was coffee. The crop till then was grown in the area for self-consumption though in other parts of Wayanad coffee plantation was an organised activity. The ongoing collective effort to gain permanent right over the land generated in them an array of hope that in not too distant a day the title to the land will be granted as the State government was seriously considering the adoption of land reform measures. Thus they gradually shifted to the plantation crops. This was also one of the crops, which brought prosperity to the migrants. The crop too over the years proved to be less attractive. Here again one of the main hurdles was the governmental restriction in the marketing of coffee. The monopoly procurement scheme made the Coffee Board the sole purchaser. In addition there was a number of other regulations. Prior permission was to be procured for marketing coffee by submitting the T P 3 form indicating the number of bags, the details of vehicle, the place where it was processed etc. If the vehicle breaks down on the way the process has to be repeated. All this was irritating and cumbersome to the farmers. Also there occurred substantial loss of plant due to plant disease. Disillusioned by all this most of them removed the plants. Even elephants were employed to remove the plants. Most significant of all the development in agriculture was the development of pepper cultivation. Here also the nature's bounty was so immense that an unprecedented prosperity resulted to the farmers. It was the golden era for Pulpally farmers and it started from mid 1980's. In quality Pulpally pepper reigned supreme and commanded premium in the market. There was no comparison as far as the yield level was concerned. Price was also at its peak. There is no exaggeration; the prosperity was so high that when one of the farmers went to a distant market to sell pepper in a jeep he had a quarrel with the jeep driver (the driver was also its owner). On the spot the jeep was purchased and the owner-driver was forced to return in a bus. The prosperity earned Pulpally various titles such as Wayanadinte Thilakakkuri, Dubai of Kerala and the Land of Black Gold. With this the face of Pulpally village underwent change and gave it a prosperous look. Most of the old houses were demolished and in its place new palatial houses came up. Consumerism was also at its peak and it was said that in terms of number of jeeps Pulpally topped then. As a corollary to all this developed trade, transport, communication and entertainment. Pepper associated prosperity also later on turned out to be somewhat elusive as there was substantial crop loss due to plant disease known as dhruthavattom. Many of the fields also turned out to be barren as the pepper plants disappeared. Cultivators have now learnt from their experience that undue dependence on single crop involves large risk. Thus a mixed cropping pattern is now a days emerging and the combination is ginger, turmeric, elephant yam, coconut, areca nut, coffee etc. Still the importance of pepper can be deduced from

Table 5.2

Total area under plantation in Pulpally

Crops	Area in acres	Percentage
Coffee	620	6.61
Rubber	500	5.33
Coconut	160	1.70
Pepper	7900	84.22
Aracanut	200	2.13
Tea	-	-
Cardamom	-	-
Total	9380	100.00

(Compiled from the village records)

Table 5.2 in which the area under plantation in the village is shown. As can be seen from the table 84.22 percent of the area under plantation is claimed by pepper followed by coffee 6.61 percent and rubber 5.33 percent. Other plantation crops of coconut and areca nut are of less significance. While this is the pattern indicated by the official statistics our data is considerably at variance. The data on cropping pattern of the respondents is shown in Table 5.3. As can be observed from the table on drylands the dominant crop is pepper, which claimed 56.16 percent of the total area. This was followed by ginger 10.63 percent, coffee 8.14 percent, areca nut 7.09 percent, rubber 5.64 percent and elephant yam 5.12 percent. In the case of wetland slightly less than 50 percent of the total area was devoted for paddy followed by areca nut 23.08 percent ginger 14.29 percent, banana 9.34 percent and elephant

Table 5.3

Cropping pattern of the respondents

Crops	Dry land Area (acres)	%	Wet land Area (acres)	%	All Area (acres)	%
Pepper	428	56.16	-	-	428	5.34
Paddy	-	-	85	46.70	85	9.00
Rubber	43	5.64	-	-	43	4.56
Banana	-	-	17	9.34	17	1.80
Ginger	81	10.63	26	14.29	107	11.33
Elephant yam	39	5.12	12	6.59	51	5.40
Arecanut	54	7.09	42	23.08	96	10.16
Coconut	31	4.07	-	-	31	3.28
Coffee	62	8.14	-	-	24	2.54
All	762	100.00	182	100.00	944	100.00

(The cropping pattern of few respondents were not available)

yam 6.59 percent. Thus what emerges from the above is that in the cropping pattern pepper continues to be dominant. In this context one of the significant development we noticed during the fieldwork is that the price fall of rubber has led to the abandonment of the plants. Quite interestingly on the rubber tree pepper plant is being grown now a days. Of late we have also been able to learn that pepper cultivation is again getting revived.

While this is one dimension of the development on the agricultural front another is maximisation of the agricultural income by way of intensive land use. Thus our data revealed that on an average a farmer in the village is able to generate out of commercial farming a gross income of Rs. 54280 per acre. After meeting the expenses there was a net income of Rs. 23461 per acre. This is inspite of a depressed market for the agricultural products of the State. Apart from this there are a variety of subsistence crops grown by the households. Our field observation revealed that most of the households has made optimum use of the land by growing commercial and subsistence crops. It can also reasonably be stated that in a significant number of cases land use exceed the optimum and it is doubtful whether this level of an intensive land use at the micro level is observable anywhere else in Kerala. On the whole suffice to state that agricultural sector in the village is most developed.

Economic Diversification

On the economic front while an intensive agricultural practice is one dimension diversification of the economy is the other. Dairy and animal husbandry has emerged as another important economic activity of the Pulpally village. Here it may be stated that though there was large-scale cattle population there are distinguishing features to the present dairy economy of the village. One is the ownership of the crossbreed cows as opposed to the traditional varieties. Secondly as against domestic use now cattle are reared for commercial purposes. Thirdly ownership cut across communities. On its size as per the Panchayat records there were 8165 cattle (cross breed 5015) in the Pulpally panchayat. This gives 0.27 cattle per 1 person. In addition there were 2387 calf, 2373 bulls, 956 buffalos, 4500 goats, 4000 pigs, 26708 hens and 500 cross bread hens in the Panchayat in 1996. As to its role it has also been indicated that 40 percent of the population of Pulpally found mainstay by dairying and animal husbandry. Though this is considerably an overestimate it can safely be said that in a number of households dairying and animal husbandry has emerged as one of the important sources of income particularly among the weaker and middle sections of the society. In the case of others it was a supplementary source of income.

In the development of trade, transport, hotel and restaurant the village witnessed profound progress. As to the size of development a brief note is made in an ensuing paragraph. As far as industrial development is concerned as is the case with the district in general the village is more backward. As per the Panchayat statistics there were 39 small-scale units out of which 22 units were of the brick making and industrial workshop type. They were giving employment to 177 persons. In addition to this there were 63 household units mostly of the traditional type making baskets out of bamboo reed, black smithy and gold smithy. The three categories accounted for 35 out of 63 household units. All the units put together provided employment to 157 persons. Thus it can be said that though not sizable there was some diversification in employment in the village over the years. To provide some idea about the level of diversification let us consider the occupational distribution of the workforce of the sample households. The same is shown in Table 5.4. It can be discerned from the table that only 17 percent of them found employment outside agriculture.

Development of Market for Agricultural Products

Markets play a crucial role for rural transformation particularly in an agriculturally developed village like

Table 5.4

Occupational distribution of workforce

Nature of occupation	Number	Percentage
Cultivation	458	50.95
Agricultural labour	288	32.04
Govt. and other organised employment	43	4.78
Business	10	1.11
Tailoring	11	1.22
Others	89	9.90
All	899	100.00

Pulpally. Agricultural production and productivity depends on the availability of inputs including credit. So also there is the need for a competitive market for agricultural products. All this plays a crucial role in determining the farm income and surplus. This in turn paves the way for rural diversification. Thus growing farmers income mean a diversified demand for non-farm goods and this in turn act as catalyst for the development of industry, services etc. On many of these counts the development course of Pulpally amply testify the importance of market. In the early fifties came up the first shop in Pulpally to sell the essential goods. Goods were brought by head load from Panamaram. Market oriented production pattern which was a later development led in turn to the progress of trading activity within the village for all the products. Today there are a number of wholesale purchasers for most of the agricultural products (hill products) grown in the area. More importantly products from neighbouring villages too comes to Pulpally. Further we have been able to learn that even from some of the production centres of the neighbouring Kannur district farmers comes to Pulpally to sell pepper. Thus Pulpally has become one of the important trading centres for agricultural products like pepper, ginger, turmeric and coffee. The traders have direct contacts with the main trading centre of the state i.e. Cochin. While this is one part of the market development the other is the establishment of a number of retail outlets for almost all the goods and services within the village. It was so diversified that now except automobiles and some of the most modern consumer durable goods a number of shops offering varied products have come to function in the area. To make a factual observation on this market development we have collected data pertaining to the number of members of the commerce and trade associations of Pulpally. The nature and size of

Table 5.5

Nature of business establishments in Pulpally

Nature of business	Number	Percentage
Purchase of agri products	87	22.31
Textiles	20	5.13
Hardwares	8	2.05
Hotels	16	4.10
Grocery/ bakery/vege table/ vending	87	22.31
Financing	8	2.05
Miscellaneous	164	42.05
All	390	100.00

establishments is shown in Table 5.5. It can be observed from the table that there were 390 members with the organisation and more than one fifth of them (22.31 percent) were the wholesale purchasers of agricultural products. An equal proportion was dealing in retail the grocery items, bakery and vegetables. What is significant to mention here is that even this number is considerably on the lower side, as there are numerous traders who are non-members of the association. Also a majority operating outside the town area are non-members. Besides almost all the petty trading establishments can be said as non-members. On the whole it is doubtful whether any other village in the whole of the Malabar area can claim so fast a development in trade and commerce made by the Pulpally village.

Needless to state monetisation of the economy naturally followed along this course of development.

Land Market

A highly developed agrarian economy is characterised by the existence of market for land. Looked from this perspective too it can be seen that the village is highly developed as there is a developed market for land. Further the price of land too has gone up by leaps and bounds in the village. To provide an insight into this we have collected the data in respect of the land disposal from the sample households. The incidence is shown in Table 5.6. As is observable from the table 102 respondents (26.77 percent) disposed land to the extent of 291.08 acres giving on an average 2.85 acres of disposal per respondent. The incidence was more common among the migrants as 35.05 percent disposed land on an average 3.64 acres. While the

Table 5.6

Incidence of land disposal

Category	No	Area (acres)	Average (acres)
Migrants	68	247.52	3.64
Chetties	26	41.08	1.58
Tribals	8	2.48	0.31
All	102	291.08	2.85

incidence among the Chetties was 27.08 percent (an average disposal of 1.58 acres) it was the lowest 8.79 percent among the tribes who disposed on an average 0.31 acre. The period wise picture shown in Table 5.7 is much more revealing. As is discernable from the table on an average the per acre cost came to Rs. 60047. Most of the transactions, 28 out of 52 (53.85 percent) occurred in the 1990's. The average value was sharply on the rise as the land cost per acre which was Rs 490 in the early

Table 5.7

Period wise incidence of land disposal

Period	No	Area (acres)	Value (Rs)	Value per acre (Rs)
Upto 1970	6	17.40	8526	490
1971-75	3	4.60	24000	5217
1976-80	4	9.50	100975	10629
1981-85	3	6.00	187500	31250
1986-90	8	12.90	649850	50376
1991-95	12	7.46	701996	94101
1996 onwards	16	7.76	2267425	292194
All	52	65.62	3940272	60047

1970's sharply rose to Rs.292194 by 1996 a rise of 596.3 times. It is further observable that the price of land in the late 1996 rose more than 3 times compared to the 1991-95 price. The practice of tenancy too can be considered as reflective of the existence of a land market. In the village tenancy is very much in practice. Our household level sample survey revealed that out of 381 households 31 households (8.14 percent) had taken land on lease to the extent of 45.21 acres giving on an average leased in land of 1.46 acres per tenant. At the same time another 28 households (7.35 percent) leased out land to the extent of 25.18 acres giving an average leased out land of 0.90 acre per household. On net basis it was found that 20.03 acres of land was leased in among the sample households and this worked out to 1.67 percent of the total owned area.

Labour Market

Labour market constitutes one of the most important institutions in the rural economy as wage labour constitutes the sustenance to many in rural areas. This is another facet of development consequent upon migration. At the time of migration what prevailed was an interlocked social structure in which a system for product sharing and offer of services was practised. Agricultural labour was also attached with the cultivators. In the system even the scope for the practice of hired labour was almost absent, not to speak of a labour market. In the initial phase of migration the need for hired labour was not very much felt as subsistence farming continued for some more time. In the next phase, which was marked by commercialisation, there was the need for hired labour to clear the forests and to develop the land. The strategies evolved by the migrants succeeded in altering the prevalent system.

Hired labour practice came into existence and as against kind payment cash wage system too was introduced. Thus there was the monetisation of the labour market. Supply mainly came from the tribal households. Gradually several forms of labour contract came into existence. The first was cash wage system in which usually for a day's work may or may not include the provision of food by the employer. There was also another practice of permanent labour according to which labour used to be employed by the farmer on a permanent basis. Further there was the share contract under which the labour received a share of the product. The practice was widely prevalent in the initial years of migration as land clearing involved sizable labour employment. This was also a reverse type where the migrants with less land had taken up the undeveloped land from the tribes and Chetties for cultivation. A share of the product belonged to the landowner. Land was taken mostly adjacent to the land of the cultivator.

Over the years the demand for labour has increased perceptibly and there are several reasons to this. Changes in cropping pattern and maintenance of plantation crops required large labour. More and more areas were also brought under cultivation by clearing the forests. A sizeable part of the surplus came to be invested by the farmers for land development and all this meant steadily rising demand for labour. At the same time forces have started operating restricting the supply of labour. As migrants experienced large economic prosperity first there was the withdrawal of women labour force from work. As status steadily improved, from the middle and large land owning classes again there was withdrawal from work by the male. Thus there was labour scarcity and rising labour cost. The wage rate in the village is now more or less comparable to the rate in advanced agricultural regions of the State and the labour has also come to enjoy considerable bargaining power. While this is an important development in the labour market the existence of a diversified market for labour is another. Thus in the initial years the demand for labour was exclusively for agricultural labour. Growing prosperity meant demand for labour of other categories mainly for building construction. As local availability was practically non existent there was immigration of labour. Rising wage rate also led to the immigration of farm labour. Thus today the economy of the village to some extent can be said as depended upon the supply of labour from the neighbouring states of Karnataka and Tamil Nadu. While a section that is from far off places camps in the village a number of labour of both sex from the neighbouring Karnataka village daily commute for work. On the whole the market oriented farming system gave way for the development of a labour market. A labour market is also functioning in the villege. In the morning labour assemble in the town, mainly migrant labour and the employers come and pick up the requisite number striking the wage deal. While this is for construction labour to some extent this is practiced by the agriculture labour too. In passing to mention the small and marginal cultivators have found such a labour market development as impinging upon them. Hence the system of Mattalpani to which a reference has been made in an earlier chapter is being practiced. This is done to reduce the employment of hired labour.

Institutional Development

Mention may also be made of certain institutions that came up in the village as they played a decisive role in the orderly development of the community and the village. An examination of this in a historical perspective will reveal who pioneered in the development of these institutions.

Pulpally Panchayat

Most important development on the institutional front is the formation of the Pulpally panchayat in 1962. The most outstanding feature was that the Panchayat functioned above party politics and narrow sectarian interests in the initial years of its formation. Thus when the first election to the Panchayat was held in 1963 there was six members out of whom 5 were Christians. Though the Christians were in majority the first President was Guru Mallappa Chetty, a Hindu. On personal reasons the President vacated the post and thereafter one Mr P C Michael master was elected as the President. He too resigned within 6 months. Then came Sri K U Matthai who continued for 16 years as the President of the Panchayat. Initially most of the people were reluctant to occupy the position, as it was a challenging job. On the developmental front responsibilities were many. At the same time there was acute scarcity of resource. Further they also found that by engaging in public affairs it was difficult to manage their own farm. The then problem was such that they have to walk 15 kms to attend the meeting of the Panchayats and hence many evinced little interest. No matter Sri Matthai took it as a challenge and made significant leap forward in the development of infrastructure facilities under the aegis of the Panchayat. In 1977 by bifurcating the Pulpally panchayat constituted the Mullankolly Panchayat. The Pulpally Panchayat has come of age and today it has emerged as the special grade Panchayat. There are now 22 wards. Since 1981 the Panchayat functions in its own building.

Pulpally Grama Survodaya Sangh

The Bhoodan movement initiated by Vinobha Bhave too made an impact in this remote village. It was the establishment of the Survodaya Sangh and under its aegis the scheme for land distribution. The Kuppothodu family laid the seeds for the movement. In 1953 when Vinobha Bhave visited Kerala in memory of his visit Kuppothodu Lakshmy Amma and her husband Ambalappady Kunhi Raman Nair donated 150 acres of land in Pulpally for distribution for the landless. Later in 1954 when Jayaprakash Narayan visited Wayanad another 100 acres was also made available. In addition to this another 36 acres of land too came into the possession of the Sangh for distribution. The Sangh, which was functioning at Kozhikode under the well known Survodaya leader Sri. Kelappan authorised Sri Kunjan Moopan and R N Kuppathodu to act as the custodians of the land. There was some delay in registering the land and the boundary was also not demarcated. It was a time when land encroachment was going on in several parts of Pulpally. The land was also not spared and 5 to 10 acres were grabbed by a number of migrants. When it was brought to the notice of the police though a number of them were evicted they continued to occupy the land. Thereafter the local leaders met the state organisers and apprised them of the development. A meeting of the concerned parties were held and the encroachers were apologetic as far as their action was concerned. Taking into account the nature of their problem it was agreed to provide 1 acre each to the encroachers. By 1961 the land was formally made available for distribution and thus 50-acres were distributed to 50 migrants. A number of them encroached more than one acre. A survey of land was conducted in 1963 and some more land was distributed. In the same year a Grama Sabha was convened and a society was formed. War on Want, a London based Society donated Rs. 6000 to the Sangh and with the same amount 4 wells and an office building was constructed for the Society in 1966. The Society also demarcated 16 acres for common purposes. Not much headway in the professed objectives the Society could accomplish on their own due to paucity of funds. Still in 1971 by availing the assistance of the Block the Society constructed 15 houses and handed over the same to the tribal people of the area. A nursery school was also opened for them with the assistance of the Tribal Development Department. The progress of the Society was later retarded, as there was difference of opinion over the issue of land encroachment. Subsequently also encroachment occurred and now the Society has 1 acre land where it is housed. It is not very active and the Board functions with Chamappara Joseph as President. The Christians also dominate it, as 5 out of 9 board members were Christians.

Development of Co-operative Institutions

Co-operatives have played a significant role in the development of the village economy, as is the case elsewhere. Let us also make a note on this development.

Pulpally Service Co-operative Bank

The Pulpally Service Co-operative Bank pioneered in the development of co-operatives in the village. It has its origin in 1921 when 30 members formed an Eikiya Nanaya Bank with Sri T V Kunhi Raman Nair as the President. From 1948 to 1972 the President was the Manager of the devaswom Sri Kuppathodu Madhavan

Nair. In 1964 it was upgraded to the status of a Service Co-operative Bank. From 1972 Sri K U Matthai (who was also the President of the Panchayat for 16 years) was elected unanimously as the President and he continues as the President since then. Though from the beginning for a considerable length of time it remained dormant later the society made dynamic growth. The society is now functioning in a building of its own constructed at a cost of Rs. 5 lakhs. The society has a working capital of Rs. 11 crores and emerged as one of the best service co-operative bank in the district enjoying special grade status.

Pulpally Milk Producers Co-operative Society

As mentioned in an earlier chapter dairy has become an important economic activity in the village and has started playing an important role in sustaining the lives of many. Needless to state the establishment of the Co-operative Society which came into existence in 1971 facilitated this. The Society has a membership of 2018 in 1998-99 and there were 2250 cattle with the members. The society has 24 collection centres within the village and in 1998-99 collected 14.23 lakh litres of milk from the producers. To comment on the role of the society out of this collection 1.39 lakh litres (9.77 percent) were only locally distributed and the balance was sold to the Union. Thus the village has become one of the largest surplus milk producing centres in the region. The Society is one among the milk societies enjoying the special status in the State, perhaps the only one in the district.

A number of other Co-operative institutions too have been found in the village. To mention there are Girijan Co-operative Society, Housing Society, Animal

Welfare Society, Agricultural Produce Marketing Society, Co-operative Hospital etc. Altogether it is said that there were nearly 18 co-operative institutions in the village. Though many are dormant what is significant to note here is that as far as development of co-operatives at the community level are concerned the village has made remarkable progress.

Social and Political Development

Migration has also brought about notable changes on the social structure, cultural and political front. A brief mention to this may now be made.

On the social front the one significant development was the gradual elimination of untouchability. Instrumental to this were the migrants. As stated above the tribal population remained untouchable in the pre-migration days and were more or less attached with the Chetty households. The locals were also reluctant to have direct contact with the migrants. This rigid social division gradually disappeared for which the migrants evolved strategies. The migrants treated the tribes equally. Accordingly they were admitted in the house and food was served in vessels. To some extent it can also be stated that they were over enthusiastic in giving an equal treatment as it constituted one of the strategies to attract the tribal labour for clearing the forest and land development. This had a telling effect on the Chetty households that an extreme form of untouchability they were not able to practice. Gradually tribes were permitted on the veranda and started serving food in vessels by the Chetties. Now a number of Chetties permit the tribes to enter the house and an equal treatment is given on occasions of marriage feast. To some extent it can be said that in the case of

Paniyas, who are in the bottom of the social ladder some discrimination and exclusion is practiced even now. At the same time with the development of labour market the age-old slavery system has almost come to an end. No longer the tribes are tied to any households.

On the religious side the Christians suffered a lot by the absence of Church in the beginning. Over the years in terms of the development of religious institutions they have recreated their own native villages in Pulpally. There are around 10 Churches in the village and in most of the corners crosses are being erected. The splendour and gaiety with which some of the religious functions are organised today they excel. The Muslims have also set up two mosques in the village.

Another notable change is the loosening of the rigid religious/caste outlook of the natives. Most of the old beliefs like sorcery, witchcraft, etc, disappeared. To state even the Daivomkanal, which was an important religious function, has become rare now. The change that occurred in the institution of marriage is the most conspicuous. Following the Christian practice dowry system has come to be in practice among the Hindus including the Chetty households. Females have now an equal share in the property. From 7 days marriage it has come to be restricted to 1 day again following the alien custom. Though among the Chetties even now marriage is held at the bridegroom's house the bride and the party now a days come only in the marriage day. They have also given up the old custom to dress like Siva and Parvathy for the marriage. Most significant social change in respect of the institution of marriage is the rising social acceptability of inter-religious/caste marriages. We came across in our sample 12 cases of mixed marriages (3.14 percent of the sample households). Out of 12 cases 6 were Christian-Hindu alliances (some including forward caste Hindus) and one Christian-Muslim alliance. The balance 5 cases were intercaste marriage within the Hindu households. Out of 12 cases 11 alliances were between the migrants and the locals. Notably even mixed marriages occurred among the tribes as there were 4 such cases involving 4 tribal girls. While 2 of them were married by Christian boys 2 were married by ezhavas. Some of them are even accommodated within the Tribal colony and this points out that there is some social acceptability to the mixed marriage. Even one arranged inter caste marriage we came across among the Hindu community involving the local and the migrant households. On this another notable development we came across is the move on the part of the Chetties to develop a broad community platform for marriage alliances by giving up the age old custom of inter group barrier. This too indicates that religious/ caste feelings have loosened.

On the social front another notable change is the nuclearisation of families. Among the Chetties the practice of Marumakkathayam has gone up and Makkathayam is practised with a tendency for more of nuclear families. Among the tribes also the earlier cohesiveness and strong bondage within the colony has vanished and side-by-side the role of the Moopan had eroded. His role is now a days confined to marriage occasions and in performing the customary practices at the family temple for the Kuladaivom.

To what extent there was adoption of the alien practices can best be indicated by the adoption of food habits. Beef was forbidden in the menu of the locals in the beginning. Now it has become the most delicious menu invariably of all the categories with the exception of Brahmins.

Attitudinal change is another one. A desire for self-improvement among the Chetties in particular is clearly visible. Attitude to education has undergone change. Even girls are now being sent for education at far off places. All of them are also more concerned about the material conditions of life. Laziness is giving way for hard work for improving the material conditions of life. The adoption of new crops and cultivation practices by the Chetties are sufficient proof to this. Though limited such impact is also felt on the tribes too. All of them acknowledged that the greatest advantage of migration was that they too learnt about new crops and cultivation practices.

At the same time it is also a fact that the relationship of the several communities with the temple, which was more intimate, has become remote. Customary practices and community privileges no longer exist and most of them have come to be reckoned as one among the participants. Thus an involvement in the activities is badly lacking among them.

On the political front the migrants were in the forefront in giving life to the political movement in the area. In general the outlook of the people changed in tune with the circumstances. The overriding consideration was their personal and social betterment. Thus in the initial phase political mobilisation was less as they hardly found time. However, the need was felt for the mobilisation of people to fight for the common cause against eviction and in this political support was decisive. In such issues also as the status being tenant cultivators the sympathy towards them came from the Communist party. Accordingly the allegiance of most of them has gone on the lines as it enabled them to be projected as an issue of the working class. No doubt this has gone a long way in earning the title to the land. Over the years large-scale prosperity resulted to the farmers. Their status also found tremendous improvement as already evidenced in an earlier chapter. Thus in accordance with this the political outlook of the people also found a U turn. The Congress party came to be favoured by most of them, as they no longer wish to be identified as belonging to the working class. This continues even now and best testimony to this is the fact that the Congress led front controls the Panchayat since contest in election started on political basis.

Absorption

The migrants are usually confronted with problems at the host place. While hostility of the natives is one problem the other is that of absorption. In the present case given the backward nature of the natives and the level of their conservatism the problem can be said as all the more serious. However, quite surprisingly the experience of the Pulpally migrants was altogether different. Though they were subjected to isolation in the initial years the phenomenon disappeared gradually and they became fully absorbed in the village and faced no hostility. This was inspite of the existence of factors conducive for the flaring up of hostility. For instance there were several cases of land disputes between the migrants and the native population as the migrants encroached the land. The large-scale encroachment over the temple land and in the consequent eviction proceedings the natives could have taken the side of the temple to their advantage. The natives however remained silent spectators being submissive and generous. Thus there was harmonious existence between the two communities. On the one hand the submissive and generous character of the local Chetties, facilitated this. On the other hand the migrants were very dominating type and also very diplomatic in their dealings with the natives. Further as the migrants had overtaken numerically they have been able to shape the social, religious, cultural and economic life of the village in tune with their own. On the whole thus they have replicated their own villages in the host place. Thus they fully got absorbed and the alien feeling vanished within a short period. This is most conspicuous from the identity they now maintain as all of them are identified as the natives of Pulpally. Accordingly when going to Travancore while in the past they said as going to the native place now they say as going to Travancore.

On the whole based on some of the factual evidences presented above and also on our impressionistic note we are to state that the development made by the village on all fronts was not only commendable but unique too. As perceptibly put by a prosperous migrant the transformation was from a state of hell to a state of heaven and hence they experienced both hell and heaven on earth. What contributed for the development is self explanatory from above. It was a migration-associated change. But what is important to reckon here is that though a number of villages witnessed large-scale in-migration this level of development was not witnessed by any of them. Precisely this necessitates mention about the distinguishing features of the Pulpally migrants. They were hard working and daring. The hardships they had undergone in the beginning and what they accomplished now in the village amply prove how daring and hardworking they were. They were also people with vision and a plan. Thus first they concentrated on the development of their own farm. Along with this some attention was paid for the peripheral development of common facilities like roads, schools, churches etc. In the next phase they worked collectively for the overall development of the village. They had unfailing unity and a few of them emerged as leaders. There was propitious environment too for them to develop these qualities. The eviction proceedings called for unity to fight back and in the process naturally some of them emerged as leaders. A number of them had also determination and pursuance. An incident is illustrative of this. As mentioned above in the course of the infrastructure development they felt that without governmental intervention not much could be accomplished. Thus the need to send a local representative to the State Assembly to muster the much-needed governmental action was felt. They vigorously pursued the idea. A young and fairly educated person belonging to the Tribal community was identified and contacted. He was reluctant, as he was about to join the government service as a teacher. This they sensed as a hindrance to his candidature. With K U Matthai, the Panchayat President in the forefront they evolved a strategy of their own. They met the Bishop at Thalassery and apprised him of their problems and plans. The solution was to provide employment to the identified person in one of the schools run by the Church in the area. The Bishop agreed to the proposal. The person was thereafter persuaded and this was how they sent their own representative to the Assembly. No doubt they succeeded in accomplishing some of their wishes as infrastructure development got a boost. How determined, persuasive and calculative they were can be gauged from the strategy they evolved and worked it out. What is remarkable is that in the forefront of all this was the Christian community. Apart from dynamism of the migrants it also need to be stated that the naxal incident too (a specific reference to this is made later) turned out to be a blessing in disguise. Some of the infrastructure like roads, communication, police station etc. got developed as a result of the incident. Here it may also be mentioned that in laying the foundation for development the contribution made by the Manager of the temple Sri Madhavan Nair was remarkable. For most of the public institutions the manager made the temple land available.

REFERENCES

Pulpally Panchayat, Integrated Development Record, Pulpally.

State Planning Board (1998), Economic Review, Govt. of Kerala, Thiruvananthapuram.

Chapter 6

Socio-economic Status of the Population

The economy of the village was in an underdeveloped state at the time of migration. Though primitive the people were leading a contended life uninfluenced by modern values. A semi feudalistic set up was also in existence in several of the social and economic relations among the communities. The influx of people with an alien culture and outlook occurred in this state leading to a shift in the religious composition and demographic balance of the population. It was also a turning point as far as the development of the village economy is concerned, as the immigrants were harbingers of socio-economic change in the village. How far such changes have been felt across the various communities is an important issue to ponder over. This chapter attempts to portray this aspect with reference to the socio-economic conditions of the households. A look into the socio-economic conditions can also throw some light on the impact of migration in the light of the pre migration review of the social and economic conditions of the people. To get a perspective on all this the households are categorised as natives and migrants. The natives are further sub-classified as Chetties and Tribes.

Demographic and Social Features

The average household size is shown in Table 6.1. The total population among the sample households worked out to 2071. This gives an average household size of 5.44 among the three categories of households. The tribal households had the highest household size of 5.75. This was followed by the migrant households, 5.43.

Table 6.1

Household size

Category	No of persons	Household size
Migrants	1053	5.43
Chetties	495	5.16
Tribals	523	5.75
All	2071	5.44

The lowest household size was among the Chetty households, 5.16. The total population comprised of 1073 males and 998 females giving a sex ratio of 930 females per 1000 males. The sex ratio is shown in Table 6.2. The

Table 6.2

Sex ratio

	Number of persons			
Category	Male	Female	Total	Sex ratio
Migrants	541	512	1053	946
Chetties	265	230	495	867
Tribals	267	256	523	959
All	1073	998	2071	930

sex ratio was low among all the category of households. The highest was among the tribal households (959) followed by the migrant households (946) and the Chetty households (867). Thus the proportion of females was the lowest among the Chetties and highest among the tribal households. The age composition of the population is shown in Table 6.3. The table reveals that more than a quarter (27.42 percent) was in the up to

Table 6.3

Age composition of the population

Age group (Years)	Migrants		Chetties		Tribals		Total	
	No	%	No	%	No	%	No	%
Upto 5	98	9.31	42	8.48	83	15.87	223	10.76
6-17	124	11.78	107	21.62	114	21.79	345	16.66
18-30	384	36.47	149	30.10	193	36.90	726	35.05
31-45	152	14.43	97	19.60	77	14.72	326	15.74
46-60	174	16.52	57	11.52	37	7.07	268	12.94
61 +	121	11.49	43	8.69	19	3.63	183	8.84
All	1053	100.00	495	100.00	523	100.00	2071	100.00

17 age group. In the 18-30 age group belonged the highest proportion, 35.05 percent followed by 15.74 percent in the 31-45 age group, 12.94 percent in the 46-60 age group and 8.84 percent in the older age group of above 61 years. Apparently the proportion of old age population was low in the village. Category wise the age composition of the households is at variance. In the scheduled tribe households there was the largest proportion of population in the younger age group up to 17 as 37.66 percent were in the age group. At the

same time in the chetty and migrant households the proportion was 30.10 and 21.09 percent respectively. Evidently among the native population the proportion of teenage population was high compared to the migrant households. The proportion of population in the 18-30 age group was high, 36.90 percent among the tribes. In the migrant households also the proportion was more or less same, 36.47 percent. Where as among the Chetty households the proportion was only 30.10 percent. At the same time the proportion of population in the 31-60 age group was lowest, 21.79 percent among the tribes. In the case of the other two categories the proportion was more or less identical, 31.12 percent and 30.95 percent respectively in the Chetty and the migrant households. The proportion of aged was also lowest 3.63 percent in the tribal category and was highest 11.49 percent in the migrant category. In the Chetty households the proportion was 8.69 percent. If we consider the economically active age group as 18-60 it can be seen that the proportion was low, 58.69 percent in the Tribal households followed by 61.22 percent in the Chetty households. The proportion was highest, 67.42 percent in the migrant households. Evidently those in the dependent age group was highest in the tribal households and lowest in the migrant households, the Chetty households being placed in the middle position.

Let us now consider the marital status as it is an important indicator of the social status of the population particularly the females. The marital status by sex is shown in Table 6.4. The status presented in the table are those who are in the age group above 18 years. The status of females stood better than males as the married constituted 72.40 percent for females against 66.88 percent for males. While 29.80 percent of males were

Table 6.4
Marital Status

Status	Number of persons		Percentage	
	Male	Female	Male	Female
Migrants				
Married	280	280	64.37	70.71
Unmarried	141	91	32.41	22.98
Widower/Widowed	14	23	3.22	5.81
Divorced	-	2	-	0.51
Total	**435**	**396**	**100.00**	**100.00**
Chetties				
Married	117	116	63.93	71.16
Unmarried	59	30	32.24	18.40
Widower/Widowed	7	14	3.83	8.59
Divorced	-	3	-	1.84
Total	**183**	**163**	**100.00**	**100.00**
Tribals				
Married	126	126	76.82	77.77
Unmarried	33	21	20.12	12.96
Widower/Widowed	1	13	0.60	8.02
Divorced	4	2	2.44	1.23
Total	**164**	**162**	**100.00**	**100.00**
All				
Married	523	522	66.88	72.40
Unmarried	233	142	29.80	19.69
Widower/Widowed	22	50	2.81	6.93
Divorced	4	7	0.51	0.97
Total	**782**	**721**	**100.00**	**100.00**

unmarried the proportion of unmarried females was only 19.69 percent. At the same time the proportion of widowed was high, 6.93 percent while the proportion of widower was only 2.81 percent. It can also be seen that the rate of divorce was comparatively high at about 1 percent for females while the ratio was 0.51 percent for males. Category wise the status makes interesting observations. Compared to other categories the marital status among the tribal appeared as better as 76.82 percent of males and 77.77 percent of females were married while the status of males in the migrant households was 64.37 percent and 63.93 percent among the chetties. Compared to migrant households the marital status of females was high, as 71.16 percent of chetties were married while the rate was 70.71 percent for migrant households. The unmarried was lowest among the tribes, 20.12 percent of males and 12.96 percent of females and it was highest among the migrants 32.41 percent for males and 22.98 percent among the females. At the same time the share was 32.24 percent of males and 18.40 percent of females in the Chetty households. The rate of widowed was high 8.59 percent among the Chetties while the proportion was 8.02 percent among the Tribal households. The proportion was only 5.81 percent among the migrants. Thus among the natives the widowhood was high. The widowers were also significant as the rate was 3.83 percent among the Chetties followed by the migrants 3.22 percent. The rate was lowest 0.60 percent among the Tribes. It is also notable that compared to the migrants the rate of divorce was high among the locals as the rate was 2.44 percent of males and 1.23 percent of females among the Tribal households against none reported among the migrants. Where as in the case of females the rate among the Chetties was relatively high

1.84 percent and the lowest 0.51 percent was among the migrants. In this context it will also be interesting to look at the unmarried by age. The same is shown in Table 6.5. As is observable from the table 96.14 percent of unmarried males and 95.77 percent of unmarried females belonged to the 18-30 age groups, respectively.

Table 6.5

Age distribution of the unmarried

Age group	Migrants		Chetties		Tribals		Total	
(Years)	M	F	M	F	M	F	M	F
18-30	139	88	53	28	32	20	224	136
	(98.58)	(96.71)	(89.83)	(93.33)	(96.33)	(95.24)	(96.14)	(95.77)
31-45	2	2	6	1	1	1	9	4
	(1.42)	(2.19)	(10.07)	(3.33)	(3.03)	(4.76)	(3.86)	(2.82)
46-60	-	1	-	1	-	-	-	2
	-(1.10)	-(3.33)	-	-	-	(1.41)		
All	141	91	59	30	33	21	233	142
	(100)	(100)	(100)	(100)	(100)	(100)	(100)	(100)

While 3.86 percent of males and 2.82 percent of females in respective order were in the 31-45 age group, 1.41 percent of females were in the 46-60 age group. Thus the unmarried was mostly in the young age group and the social problem of non-marital status appears as low. Among the various categories the problem was much more among the Chetties as the proportion of unmarried in the old age group was high. Thus while 6.66 percent of females and 10.07 percent of males aged above 31 years were unmarried among them the proportion was 3.03 percent of males and 4.76 percent of females in the ST households. At the same time in the migrant category the proportion was 1.42 percent among the

males and 3.29 percent among the females. Thus chetty households were less favourably placed in the marital status.

Another aspect is nuclearisation of families (Table 6.6). On an average it can be seen that joint families were high, 43.04 percent. The proportion of joint families was high 49.48 percent among the migrant households followed by 41.76 percent among Tribal households. It was considerably low at 31.25 percent among the Chetty households. Thus the joint family system appears to be high among the migrant households and less among the chetty households.

Table 6.6

Number of joint families

Category	Total	Number of joint families	Percentage
Migrants	194	96	49.48
Chetties	96	30	31.25
Tribals	91	38	41.76
All	381	164	43.04

Education

As noted above even the peripheral facilities for education available in the area was inaccessible to most of them in the beginning. With migration the scenario underwent rapid changes, as there was marked development of educational facilities. Further as noted above the migrants had the best perception about the value of education and hence evolved their own strategies in educating their wards. In fact they were ambitious that their children's fate should be different from theirs and hence best education has to be imparted to them.

To some extent this can inspire other communities too. To what extent the communities have responded can now be examined. To examine from this angle the educational level of the population is shown in Table 6.7. In the table the educational status of the population aged above 5 and who were not currently undergoing education is shown. Among the sample population it is revealing to note that 16.55 percent of the population had no formal schooling. While 36.31 percent had education up to seventh standard another 30.15 percent had education up to 10 years. Only 17 percent had education above 10th standard. Sex wise the proportion without any school education was high 21.81 percent against 11.64 percent of males. At the same time the proportion with above 10th standard education was marginally higher for females 17.42 percent while the corresponding proportion in the case of males was 16.60 percent. Category wise interesting observations can now be made. Educationally the migrants were the most advanced. Thus while the proportion of those without any formal education was only 3.81 percent among the migrant population it was 13.85 percent among the Chetties and as high as 49.02 percent among the Tribal population. Similarly it can be seen that while the proportion above tenth standard education was 26.94 percent among the migrant population the proportion with the same level of schooling was low, 10.53 percent among the Chetties and 0.28 percent among the Tribal population. As is usual the educational advancement of female population stood considerably lower than males in all categories of households. The tribal females were much more backward as 58.62 percent never had been to school.

To throw further light on this issue of social development let us consider the rate of school enrolment

Table 6.7

Educational level of the population

Livels of education	Migrants			Chetties			Tribals			All		
	Male	Female	Total	Male	Female	Total	Male	Female	Total	Male	Female	Total
Illiterates	10	22	32	10	40	50	74	102	176	94	164	258
	(2.29)	(5.44)	(3.81)	(5.35)	(22.99)	(13.85)	(40.00)	(58.62)	(49.02)	(11.64)	(21.81)	(16.55)
Upto 7	146	141	287	75	60	135	91	53	144	312	254	566
	(33.56)	(34.90)	(34.21)	(40.11)	(34.48)	(37.40)	(49.18)	(30.46)	(40.11)	(38.66)	(33.78)	(36.31)
Upto 10	168	126	294	79	59	138	20	18	38	267	203	470
	(38.62)	(31.19)	(35.04)	(42.25)	(33.91)	(38.23)	(10.81)	(10.34)	(10.58)	(33.09)	(26.99)	(30.15)
Intermediate	80	81	161	18	13	31	-	1	1	98	95	193
	(18.30)	(20.05)	(19.19)	(9.62)	(7.47)	(8.59)	-	(0.57)	(0.28)	(12.14)	(12.63)	(12.38)
Under graduation	31	34	65	5	2	7	-	-	-	36	36	72
	(7.13)	(8.42)	(7.75)	(2.67)	(1.15)	(1.94)	-	-	-	(4.46)	(4.79)	(4.62)
All	435	404	839	187	174	361	185	174	359	807	752	1559
	(100.00)	(100.00)	(100.00)	(100.00)	(100.00)	(100.00)	(100.00)	(100.00)	(100.00)	(100.00)	(100.00)	(100.00)

of the children in the eligible age group. For the same we consider the population up to the age group of 17. The enrolment rate is shown in Table 6.8. The total enrolment rate worked out to 57.57 percent in the age group we considered. The highest enrolment rate was in the 6-17 age group, 83.77 percent. In the up to 5 age group the enrolment rate worked out to 17.04 percent.

Table 6.8

Rate of school enrolment

Age group	Migrants	Chetties	Tribals	All
Upto 5	27.55	11.90	7.23	17.04
6-17	93.55	85.98	71.05	83.77
All	64.41	65.10	44.16	57.57

Category wise the Chetties and migrants were characterised by high enrolment (65.10 percent, 64.41 percent respectively). The Tribes had the lowest rate, 44.16 percent. On the whole it can be inferred from all this that the migrant population is characterised by high level of educational advancement. The Chetties followed this. Thus in educational advancement the tribal category still continue to trail far behind others.

Economic Status

Now let us make an attempt to evaluate the economic conditions of the people in the post migration period. The same is attempted with reference to the nature of work, land and other assets ownership, housing condition etc.

Work Participation Rate

The work participation rate of the population by age group is shown in Table 6.9. Among the 381

Table 6.9

Work force participation rate

Age Group (Years)	Migrants						Chetties					
	Male		Female		All		Male		Female		All	
	T	W	T	W	T	W	T	W	T	W	T	W
Upto 18	105	-	117	-	222	-	82	3	67	3	149	6
								(3.66)		(3.66)		(4.03)
18-30	205	178	179	24	384	202	81	75	68	14	149	89
		(86.83)		(13.14)		(52.60)		(92.59)		(20.59)		(59.73)
31-45	70	68	80	23	152	91	51	48	46	23	97	71
		(97.14)		(28.05)		(59.86)		(94.12)		(50.00)		(73.20)
46-60	88	80	86	16	174	96	27	25	30	4	57	29
		(90.91)		(18.60)		(55.17)		(92.59)		(13.33)		(50.88)
61+	73	25	48	3	121	28	23	10	20	1	43	11
		(34.25)		(6.25)		(23.14)		(43.48)		(5.00)		(25.58)
All	541	351	512	66	1053	417	264	161	231	45	495	206
		(64.88)		(12.89)		(39.60)		(60.98)		(19.48)		(41.62)

Table 6.9 Cont.

Age Group (Years)	Tribals						All				Grand total	
	Male		Female		All		Male		Female			
	T	W	T	W	T	W	T	W	T	W	T	W
Upto 18	103	9	94	-	197	9	290	12	278	3	568	15
	(8.74)		(4.57)		(4.14)		(1.08)		(2.64)			
18-30	92	83	101	68	193	151	378	336	348	106	726	442
	(90.22)		(67.33)		(78.24)		(88.89)		(30.46)		(60.88)	
31-45	42	40	35	33	77	73	163	156	163	79	326	235
	(95.24)		(94.29)		(94.81)		(95.71)		(48.47)		(72.09)	
46-60	21	19	16	13	37	32	136	124	132	33	268	157
	(90.48)		(81.25)		(86.49)		(91.18)		(25.00)		(58.58)	
61+	9	6	10	5	19	11	105	41	78	9	183	50
	(66.67)		(50.00)		(57.89)		(39.05)		(11.54)		(27.32)	
All	267	157	256	119	523	276	1072	669	999	230	2071	899
	(58.80)		(46.48)		(52.77)		(62.41)		(23.02)		(43.41)	

T-Total, W-Workers

households the workers constituted 899 or there was 2.36 workers per household and hence the work participation rate comes to 43.41 percent. Child labour participation rate was observed as low as 2.64 percent of persons aged up to 18 were workers. At the same time the participation rate of aged population was high, as 27.32 percent of those aged above 61 were currently workers. The highest participation rate among the workable age group was in the 31-45 age group as 72.09 percent were workers followed by 60.88 percent in the 18-30 age group and 58.58 percent in the 46-60 age group. Sex wise picture is quite revealing. The participation rate of females was low as almost one third of the rate of males (23.02 percent females and 62.41 percent males). Compared to males the incidence of female child labour practice was low as 1.08 percent of females in the up to 17 age group were working while the rate was 4.14 percent for male children. Among the females also the participation rate of aged above 61 was low 11.54 percent while the rate was more than 3 times high, 39.05 percent for males. Thus there was significant participation in work by the aged males. Among the usual workable age group the participation rate of females was high, 48.47 percent in the 31-45 age group while the corresponding rate of males was 95.71 percent. While in the case of males the next highest participation rate of 91.18 percent was in the 46-60 age group (females 25 percent) in the case of females the next highest rate was in the 18-30 age group, 30.46 percent (88.89 percent for males). Thus evidently male work participation rate varied by a wide margin from that of females in all the age groups. Category wise participation rate makes interesting reading. Tribes were characterised by high work participation rate, 52.77 percent while the rate was 41.62 percent for Chetties and 39.60 percent among the migrant households. Compared to other categories child labour participation in work was high among the Tribal households, 4.57 percent while it was 4.03 percent among the Chetty households. Among the migrant households child labour was absent. Much more significant to note is the rate of participation in work by the aged population. In the ST category the rate comes to 57.89 percent while it was 25.58 percent among the Chetties and 23.14 percent among the migrant households. In all other age groups also a similar pattern follows that the work participation rate among the Tribal population was highest compared to the population of other categories. Sex wise also interesting observations can be made. In Tribal households female work participation by the 31-45 age group was more or less comparable to that of males. Thus while in the 31-45 age group female work participation rate was 94.29 percent it was 95.24 percent for males. Where as in other age groups the female participation rate stood lower than males by a wide margin. Again coming to the Chetty households it can be seen that female work participation rate was high, 19.48 percent against 12.89 percent by the migrant households. Here it is pertinent to point out the change in the attitude towards work among the various categories. In the traditional set up the female work participation in non-household work was absent among the Chetty households and they were strictly confined to household work. However the female work participation rate has gone up in the post migration period. At the same time we have been able to note that invariably the women of the migrant households participated in farm development and cultivation in the initial stage of migration. However notably the rate has considerably dropped now. This is attributable to the change in the economic status of the households. No doubt in agriculture based rural economy with economic improvement the females withdraw from work. In the post migration period the prosperity was felt more by the migrant households compared to the natives. In fact many of the native households felt deterioration in a relative sense and on this we make a detailed comment later. Thus naturally there was withdrawal of female labour from work among the migrants and rising participation among the native population. It is again significant to note that participation rate of aged population among the ST households was high of both sex which again speak of the relative status of the tribes. On the whole it emerges that if work participation rate is any indicator of economic status the condition of tribal households was worse and the migrant households better. The Chetties occupies the middle position.

Occupational Structure

An examination of the occupational structure can provide further insight into the economic conditions of the households. The occupational structure is shown in Table 6.10. For the occupational classification of labour the employment in which they were employed for the major part of the year preceding the study was considered as the primary occupation of the respondents. Category wise it can be seen that employment was more diversified in the case of migrant households and the least diversified was among the tribal households. Further it is notable that while cultivation accounted as the dominant occupation of the migrant and Chetty households (72.90 percent and 72.82 percent respectively) 93.42 percent of the Tribal workers worked as agricultural labour. Cultivation as an occupation was reported by only 1.45 percent of the tribal workers. It can also be seen that out of 43 employed in the secured

Table 6.10

Category wise occupational distribution of work force

Nature of job	Migrants		Chetties		Tribals		Total	
	No	%	No	%	No	%	No	%
Cultivation	304	72.90	150	72.82	4	1.45	458	50.95
Agri. labour	7	1.67	23	11.17	258	93.42	288	32.04
Business	9	2.16	1	0.48	-	-	10	1.11
Govt. and other professions	31	7.43	10	4.85	2	0.72	43	4.78
Tailoring	4	0.96	7	3.38	-	-	11	1.22
Others	62	14.87	15	7.28	12	4.35	89	9.90
All	417	100.00	206	100.00	276	100.00	899	100.00

organised sector 31 (72.09 percent) were among the migrant households. Further out of 10 reported as business 9 belonged to the migrant category. Other rural non farm employment absorbed 14.87 percent of the employed among the migrant households while the proportion was 7.28 percent among Chetties and as low as 4.35 percent among the Tribes. On the whole what emerges from the above analysis is that almost all the tribes have turned out to be daily wage earners in the agricultural sector.

Current Land Ownership

In agriculturally dominated rural economy land constitutes one of the important assets of the rural households. In fact what led the people to move out permanently from the native village was the desire to own large land holdings in order to sustain the family. No surprise even it meant unscrupulous methods they came to own substantial land in the beginning. What is more relevant in examining the economic status is the current size of land ownership. The size of land ownership is shown in Table 6.11 as dry and wetland. The total landholdings of the land owning households numbering 367comes to 1194.68 acres giving an average holding of 3.26 acres per household. Here it is significant to note that 14 households was landless (3.67 percent). The total land comprised of 938.80 acres of dry land (78.58 percent) giving 3.52 acres per household and 255.88 acres of paddy field (21.42 percent) giving an average holding of 1.62 acres per household. Category wise the average landholdings of the migrants and the native Chetties more or less corresponded and was 3.86 acres and 3.77 acres, respectively. Whereas the average holding of the Tribes (1.08 acres) was less than one third of the size of landholding of the other categories.

Table 6.11

Current land ownership pattern (area in acres)

Category	Wet land			Dry land			All		
	No.	Area	Av	No.	Area	Av	No.	Area	Av
Migrants	70	67.52	0.96	194	682.08	3.52	194	749.60	3.86
Chetties	74	164.40	2.22	96	197.84	2.06	96	362.24	3.77
Tribals	13	23.96	1.84	77	58.88	0.77	77	82.84	1.08
All	158	255.88	1.62	267	938.80	3.52	367	1194.68	3.26

All the 14 landless also belonged to the tribal category. This indicates the incidence of landlessness of the magnitude of 15.38 percent among the Tribals. Further it is important to note that natives possessed more wetland - on an average 2.22 acres by the Chetties and 1.84 acres by the Tribes. At the same time the size held by the migrants was only 0.96 acres. The proportion holding the wetland is also noteworthy. While 77.08 percent of the native Chetties owned wetland the proportion was only 36.59 percent among the migrants and 14.29 percent among the Tribes. There was wide variation in the size of land ownership and to bring out this fact the distribution of households by size of landholding is shown in Table 6.12. It may be noted that the range in the size of land ownership among the households varied from 0.02 acre of garden land owned by a ST household to 27.50 acres of garden land owned by a migrant household. In the case of paddy field the range was from 0.08 acre held by a migrant to 10 acres owned by a native Chetty household. The overall range was from 0.02 acre to 30 acres. It can be seen from the table that one third of the households owned land marginal in size, less than 1 acre. While 25.89 percent held between 1.01-2.50 acres another 20.16 percent owned between 2.51-5 acres. The balance 20.17 percent owned above 5.01 acres. Category wise most of the Tribes owned land marginal in size as 77.92 percent owned less than 1 acre. At the same time the proportion of households holding the same size of land was 26.04 percent among the Chetties and 20.10 percent among the migrants. It is also significant to note that majority of Chetty households (57.29 percent) owned less than 2.50 acres while the proportion was 48.97 percent among the migrants and 89.61 percent among the Tribes. Also out of 19 persons owning above 10.01 acres 12 belonged

Table 6.12

Distribution of households by current size of land holdings

Size of land (acres)	Migrants No.	Migrants %	Chetties No.	Chetties %	Tribals No.	Tribals %	All No.	All %
Less than 1	39	20.10	25	26.04	60	77.92	124	33.79
1.01 - 2.50	56	28.87	30	31.25	9	11.69	95	25.89
2.51 - 5.00	46	23.71	22	22.92	6	7.79	74	20.16
5.01- 7.50	26	13.40	8	8.33	2	2.60	36	9.81
7.51 - 10.00	15	7.73	4	4.17	-	-	19	5.18
10.01 and above	12	6.19	7	7.29	-	-	19	5.18
All	194	100.00	96	100.00	77	100.00	367	100.00

to the migrant category. The inference that follows is clear; the size of land owned by the migrant households was high followed by the native Chetties and the Tribes. The inequality in the size of land ownership was also notable inter and intra category.

Ownership of Farm Assets

With wealth accumulation one can expect a shift from landed wealth to farm assets and live stocks. To know how far this is valid in this particular case let us consider the farm and livestock assets. The ownership of live stock assets is shown in Table 6.13. We consider the main live stock assets of bullocks, cattle and calf, goat, pig and hen. As to the pattern of holdings among the sample households 25 (6.56 percent) possessed 62 bullocks (2.48 per household), 233 households (61.15 percent of households) 372 milch cattle (1.60 per

Table 6.13

Ownership pattern of cattle and livestock assets

Items	Migrants		Chetties		Tribals		All	
	No	Total	No	Total	No	Total	No	Total
Bullocks	2	4	22	56	1	2	25	62
Milch cattle	154	245	64	107	15	20	233	372
Calf	141	205	58	77	12	23	211	305
Goat	52	142	27	81	23	81	102	304
Pig	10	22	3	4	3	3	16	29
Hen	121	750	52	365	14	72	187	1187

household), 211 households (55.38 percent of households) 305 calf (1.45 per household), 102 households (26.77 percent of households) 304 goats (2.98 per household), 187 households (49.08 percent of households) 1187 hens (6.35 per household) and 16 households (4.20 percent) 29 pigs (1.81 per household). Of all the items thus the most popular was milch cattle. Rearing hen too can be found as extensive. The pattern of ownership displayed distinct features by category of households. While 79.38 percent of migrant households possessed on an average 1.59 milch cattle the proportion of households was 66.67 percent among the Chetties (1.67 per household) and 16.48 percent among the Tribal households (1.33 per household). The Chetty households owned most of the bullocks as they owned 90.32 percent of the total bullocks. Similarly while 72.68 percent of migrant households had calf (on an average 1.45 per household) the proportion of households was 60.42 percent among the Chetties (1.33 per household) and 13.19 percent among the Tribal households (1.91 per household).

Coming to the pattern of ownership of goat it can be seen that while 26.80 percent of migrant households had the asset on an average 2.73 per household the proportion was 28.13 percent among the Chetties (3 per household) and 25.27 percent among the ST households (3.52 per household). Coming to the item hen it can again be seen that the proportion of households was 62.37 percent among the migrants (6.20 per household) while it was 54.17 percent among the Chetties (7 per household) and 15.38 per cent of Tribal households (5.14 per household). More or less it can thus be seen that in the case of most of the live stock assets the incidence of ownership and the size of assets was high among the migrant households. Possession of milch cattle was extensive among the migrants and Chetties. Ownership of goat was relatively high among the Tribes. In this context it may be noted that in the pre-migration socio-economic set up cattle was an important asset of the Chetty households. However market for milk was then absent. With migration the scenario has changed. There was growing market for milk and the setting up of the Co-operative milk society gave a big boost for the activity. Thus dairy industry has come to be adopted as an avenue to supplement the income of the households. However Tribes are handicapped to adopt dairy due to limited land ownership. Common grazing land, which was plenty in the pre-migration period, has become extinct now. Scope for grazing in the neighbourhood too has become very difficult, as there is intensive land use. Thus inspite of the development of animal husbandry and other supplementary income sources the Tribes have come to own less of such assets.

In this context it will also be interesting to look at the agricultural and allied investments. We have the data on the ownership of tractor, thriller, investment in land development and investment in manger. The data again revealed that 1 migrant and 1 Chetty household owned the tractor. In respect of thriller 2 households one each among the migrants and Chetties owned the item.

The cultivators in general have made sizable investment in land development. A major part of this investment involved employment of labour mainly family labour and hence there was not much out of pocket expenses. Further such works were undertaken over the years. Thus an estimate about this size of investment cannot be made. At the same time an attempt was made to work out the size of investment that involved out of pocket expenses from the respondents. The respondents were asked to state roughly such expenses out of memory. At the same time some of the investments, like irrigation they were able to provide more or less correctly. Thus it has to be borne in mind that the investment figures we discuss have limitations and cannot be taken as final. The results revealed that 162 households (the figures in respect of other households were not available) had invested Rs. 68.45 lakhs giving an average investment of Rs. 42253 per household. Category wise picture is shown in Table 6.14. Largest

Table 6.14

Size of investment in land development and irrigation

Category	No.of households	Amount (Rs. lakhs)	Average amount (Rs.)
Migrants	124	56.28	45384
Chetties	33	11.00	33362
Tribals	5	1.17	23362
All	162	68.45	42253

investment was undertaken by the migrants on an average Rs. 45384 by 124 migrant households. This was followed by the Chetty households Rs. 33362 on an average by 33 households and Rs. 23362 by 5 Tribal households. The migrant households made evidently most of the investments, 82.22 percent of the total. In the case of tribal households we came to notice that such investments were financed by the state under the Tribal Development Scheme.

In the course of the field investigation another allied investment that we noticed was the construction of mangers as cattle ownership has become extensive. There was subsidy scheme for the construction. Our data revealed that 108 households had made an investment of Rs. 14.91 lakhs giving an average investment of Rs. 13805 per household. Category wise disparity in investment is striking (Table 6.15) as 85 migrant households accounted for the 97.45 percent of total investment. Thus while the average investment made by them was Rs. 17,099 the investment made by the 20 Chetty households (20.83 percent) was a meagre Rs. 1553 on an average and the 3 Tribal households (3.30 percent) Rs. 2250 per household. Thus the migrant households made most of the farm investments.

Table 6.15

Size of investment in manger

Category	No. of households	Amount (Rs. lakhs)	Average amount (Rs.)
Migrants	85	14.53	17099
Chetties	20	0.31	1553
Tribals	3	0.07	2250
All	108	14.91	13805

Ownership of Consumer Durable Goods

Ownership of consumer durable goods is one of the best indicators of the economic status of the households. To provide an insight from this angle the size of ownership of selected items per 1000 households is shown in Table 6.16. As can be observed from the table the traditional items of radio and watch was owned more or less extensively as there was 2079 watches and 780 radios per 1000 households. Modern consumer durable goods were rare, as the ownership of Television

Table 6.16

Ownership of consumer durable goods (Ownership per 1000 households)

Items	Migrants	Chetties	Tribals	Total
Watch	2830	2042	516	2079
Radio	918	875	385	780
Television	469	156	11	281
Dish antenna	258	104	-	157
Washing machine	103	-	-	52
Refrigerator	180	-	-	81
Cooking gas	320	104	-	189
Telephone	232	42	-	129

was 281, 129 telephones, 157-dish antennas, 81 refrigerators and 52 washing machines per 1000 households. Category wise picture makes interesting reading. The migrant households owned most of the consumer durable goods. Thus while the ownership of television was 469 per 1000 households in the category it was 156 sets in the case of Chetties and as low as 11 (only one household out of 91) among the Tribal households. The only modern consumer durable good owned by the Tribal was the one television set. Wide inequality in the ownership of consumer durables existed between the migrants and the chetties. Thus when none of the chetty households owned refrigerator and washing machine the respective ownership was 180 and 103 per 1000 households among the migrants. Telephone ownership was 5.52 times high among the migrant households compared to the chetty households.

Coming to the cooking medium again the results indicate that while nearly a third of the migrant households owned LPG connection it was only slightly higher than one tenth among the chetty households. None of the tribal households possessed the LPG connection.

Reference can also be made on the ownership pattern of private vehicles. The ownership pattern is given in Table 6.17. Here again the emerging picture is not different. Among the total households there was 58 two wheelers, 42 jeeps, 21 cars and 13 vans per 1000 households. All of them were concentrated among the migrant households. The inference that can be drawn

Table 6.17

Ownership of private vehicles (per 1000 households)

Items	Migrants	Chetties	Tribals	Total
Two wheelers	103	21	-	58
Jeep	62	42	-	42
Car	36	10	-	21
Van	26	-	-	13

from all this is clear-the migrant households are far better placed as far as the ownership of consumer durable goods are concerned.

Housing Condition

Let us now consider the housing condition of the respondents. Roof condition of the houses can give some idea and the same is shown in Table 6.18. While nearly half of the houses were tiled, 17.32 percent of houses were fully concreted and 12.07 percent a mixture of both. The rest 20.99 percent can be said as in a poor condition. Category wise more than one fourth of the migrants owned concrete houses and another 41.24 percent tiled houses. It can be seen that 89.18 percent of migrant households had pucca houses. Whereas the proportion with pucca houses was 70.83 percent among the chetties and 65.93 percent among the Tribes. Here a particular note may have to be made about the housing condition of the Tribes. Though going by the roof condition most

Table 6.18

Distribution of households by housing condition

Items	Migrants		Chetties		Tribals		All	
	No.	%	No.	%	No.	%	No.	%
Concrete	54	27.84	8	8.33	4	4.39	66	17.32
Tiled	80	41.24	53	55.21	56	61.54	189	49.61
Concrete and tiled	39	20.10	7	7.29	-	-	46	12.07
Sheet and tiled	20	10.31	13	13.54	17	18.68	50	13.12
Thatched	1	0.51	15	15.63	14	15.38	30	7.87
All	194	100.00	96	100.00	91	100.00	381	100.00

of them have come to own tiled houses they were in a very poor condition, our visual observation revealed. Tribal houses were sponsored by the government. Thus in accordance with the specification though the houses are tiled they were invariably in a dilapidated condition. The floor condition too can be cited to strengthen this observation. Accordingly it was found that 85.71 percent of Tribal houses were cow dung polished while the proportion was 60.42 percent among the Chetties and 17.53 percent among the migrants. Evidently in the case of chetties too a significant number had very poor houses as 15.63 percent had thatched roof while the proportion was 0.51 percent among the migrants. As to the distress condition of some of the Chetties no further proof need to be searched.

Per Capita Consumption Expenditure

To further highlight the differential status we finally considered the per capita household consumption expenditure (Table 6.19). The results are further illustrative of our above observation. Taking the households as a whole it can be seen that 17.06 percent of households had per capita consumption expenditure less than Rs. 200 per month. While 43.57 percent spent between Rs. 200-400, 22.57 percent spent between Rs 400-600, 8.92 percent between Rs. 601-800 and 3.94 percent between Rs. 800-1000. In the case of 3.94 percent the per capita expenditure exceeded Rs. 1001. Thus while many are in distress a number of them are in affluence going by this size of per capita consumption expenditure. Category wise picture provides the community dimension of disparity. Thus again in tune with our above observation the Tribes and chetties were economically backward. If we consider a cut off level per capita expenditure of Rs. 200 per month as the bare minimum

Table 6.19

Distribution of households by monthly per capita consumption expenditure

Items	Migrants		Chetties		Tribals		All	
	No.	%	No.	%	No.	%	No.	%
Upto 100	1	0.51	5	5.21	9	9.89	15	3.94
101-200	10	5.15	15	15.63	25	27.47	50	13.12
200-400	62	31.96	58	60.42	46	50.55	166	43.57
400-600	61	31.44	15	15.62	10	10.99	86	22.57
601-800	32	16.49	1	1.04	1	1.09	34	8.92
801-1000	13	6.70	2	2.08	-	-	15	3.94
1001 +	15	7.73	-	-	-	-	15	3.94
All	194	100.00	96	100.00	91	100.00	381	100.00

it can be found that the expenditure of 37.36 percent of tribes stood lower than this. The proportion of households with the same expenditure was 20.83 percent among the chetty households and 5.66 percent among the migrant households. Further to cite, if we consider a per capita expenditure of Rs. 601 and above as fairly high 30.92 percent of migrant households belonged to this expenditure class. At the same time the proportion of households in the Chetty category was 3.12 percent and in the Tribal category there was 1.09 percent. As to the economic backwardness of the native population no further proof is required.

Indebtedness

The incidence of indebtedness of the households is shown in Table 6.20. Out of 381 households 270 (70.86

Table 6.20

Indebtedness of the households (Rs. lakhs)

Source	Migrants			Chetties			Tribals			All		
	No.	Amount	Average Amount	No.	Amount	Aerage Amount	No.	Amount	Average Amount	No.	Amount	Average Amount
Co-op. banks	99	35.38	0.35	42	12.40	0.30	4	0.23	0.06	145	48.01	0.33
Grameen bank	28	10.70	0.38	6	2.81	0.47	5	0.66	0.13	39	14.17	0.36
Comm. banks	96	55.83	0.58	44	25.63	0.58	12	3.46	0.29	152	84.92	0.56
L.I.C.	8	3.52	0.44	1	0.06	0.06	3	0.04	0.01	1292	3.62	0.30
Others	32	11.00	0.34	15	5.75	0.38	20	10.56	0.53	67	27.31	0.41
All	159	116.43	0.73	74	46.65	0.63	37	14.95	0.40	270	178.03	0.66

percent) were indebted on an average Rs.0.66 lakh. Largest borrowing was from commercial banks as out of 178.03 lakhs of household debt Rs. 84.92 lakhs (47.70 percent) were drawn from the banks followed by co-operative banks (26.97 percent) and other sources mainly comprised of friends, relatives and credit purchases (15.34 percent). Category wise the debt incidence can be found as high among the migrant households as 159 out of 194 (81.95 percent) were indebted while the proportion was 77.08 percent among the chetties and 40.66 percent among the tribes. The size of borrowings also follows a similar pattern as the average borrowing of the migrants was the highest Rs. 0.73 lakh followed by the Chetty households Rs. 0.63 lakh and lowest by the Tribal households Rs. 0.40 lakh. Source wise the institutional sources of borrowings was the largest, 90.56 percent of the total borrowings of the migrants and 87.68 percent by the Chetties. Quite contrary to this the non-institutional sources accounted for 70.64 percent of the total borrowings of the tribes. Being asset less no surprise the access to credit turned out to be less to the tribes. Further the incidence of indebtedness in general among the households can be seen as on the higher side. There was reason to this. As we learnt the price of pepper was found as low than they expected at the last harvest season and many farmers have mobilised funds by way of borrowings to hold the product in expectation of a high price. Also we have noted that the agricultural sector in the State is in general in the grip of recession and this too led to the phenomenon of high debt burden in the village.

On the whole it emerges that in the post migration period the development witnessed by the village was quite impressive on all fronts. However from some of the indicators of social and economic status of the various categories of households it emerges that the migrant community in general has realised the best status improvement compared to the native population. The data not presented here further revealed that among the migrants the Christian community in particular effected better status improvement compared to other communities. In education, size of land and other assets ownership, living conditions, employment structure etc. this is clearly evident. Among the native population the Chetties have somewhat improved the status though a significant number of them are in distress. Dismally it has been evidenced that the native Tribes remained by and large marginalised. Though limited educational advancement have been made by the community their economy and living conditions continue to be appalling in nature.

Chapter 7

Costs of Migration

Travancore migrants were harbingers of progress in many of the villages in Malabar. The dimensions of this development has already been depicted with reference to Pulpally. At the same time it is equally important to note that there were significant ill effects to this migration. They are multi dimensional also in nature. Further it has to be noted that in some of the villages like Pulpally in numerical strength the migrants has surpassed the native population. Thus they have come to dominate the social, economic and political life in the village. This too has generated problems. We now pass on to take stock of this negative impact of migration and the other problems that cropped up as a consequence of migration

Economic Costs

On the economic front one of the side effects of migration is the disparity in development. This is true of areas as well as classes within the village. Thus within the village there was vast disparity in the level of development between areas. This has also a community dimension as areas occupied by the native population are comparatively less developed. Most conspicuous was the disparity in the development of transport, communication and social infrastructure. This can be very well illustrated by portraying the present status of Chekady, which is a part of the Pulpally village. Chekady is located on the banks of the Kabini River. Forests surround the other three sides. There are almost 800 families living in the area. Three fourth are tribes and among the rest the Chetties dominate. It was also one of the earliest settlements in the village. In fact many of the migrants came to Pulpally via Chekady. Almost all of them accepted the hospitality of the locals and some of them even stayed a night at Chekady on their way to Pulpally. Even now the area is very backward. Though a road was constructed recently it is not fit for travel in all seasons. They have to travel on foot four to five Kms. to reach the nearest bus point. Electricity remains a far cry. The scope for its availability also appears as bleak as the lines have to pass through the forest and the much-needed co-ordination among the various governmental departments is said as lacking. Communication facilities are virtually absent as there is neither a post office nor a telephone. Postal delivery is made only once in a week. Coming to the development of educational facilities paradoxically the area became much more backward. Accordingly though in Chekady came up the first school, which got upgraded as an upper primary school at one point in time later it was downgraded to the status of a lower primary school. This status continues even today. For education above primary level children has to be send to Pullpally, which is about 8 Kms. away and the only well to do among them do so. The rest have to be contended with primary education. Though for health care provision a sub health centre was set up in the area for years it was closed for want of staff and as stated by some of them they survives on the grace of God. On the economic front paddy cultivation is the main occupational avenue. To state in the whole settlement the only person securely employed in the modern sector is a bank clerk. In off-seasons labour is recruited in – group for seasonal works in the neighbouring state of Karnataka. Though dairying holds good prospects in the area its commercial adoption is constrained by the absence of marketing facilities. The dairy co-operative has not been able to set up a procurement centre given the constraints of transport and communication. The people are even giving up the activity though in other areas of Pulpally the activity is making phenomenal progress. From our visual observation we can state that poverty is wide spread in the area across all sections and the people are leading even now somewhat a primitive life. On its present status as opined by one of the oldest persons in the area Chekady was famous in the pre migration period and now no one knows about Chekady. Mass migration has not taken place in the area, as it was individual Janmam lands and scope for encroachment was absent. Thus to conclude Chekady remains cut off from the developed part of Pulpally.

While this is the case of one of the oldest settlements, in the new settlements also development disparities are observable. The areas occupied by the migrants have well-developed roads, communication and other infrastructure facilities while in other areas development has far lagged behind. Though not to the extent of Chekady other areas called Vandikkadavu and Perikkallur mostly inhabited by locals remains still less developed compared to other areas. The availability of some of the infrastructure facilities of roads, electricity, telephone etc. among the various communities we studied shown in Table 7.1 can provide further evidence to this development disparity. As is discernable from the table among the sample households 45.41 percent had electrified houses and 60.03 percent had developed road connection. Slightly more than a tenth of the households had the telephone connection. In the case of these entire facilities category wise, the migrants are in a superior

Table 7.1

Availability of infrastructure facilities

Category	Electricity		Road		Telephone	
	No.	%	No.	%	No.	%
Migrants	127	65.46	174	89.69	45	23.19
Chetties	33	34.38	42	43.75	4	4.20
Tribals	13	14.29	15	16.48	-	-
All	173	45.41	231	60.03	49	12.86

status as most of the facilities are concentrated among them. Thus while 65.46 percent of the households were electrified and 89.69 percent had road connection among the migrants among Chetties the proportion of households with electric connection was 34.38 and road connection 43.75 percent. In respect of these two facilities the condition of tribal households was one of pathetic as only 14.29 percent of houses were electrified and 16.48 percent had road connection. Coming to telephone ownership while 23.19 percent of migrant households owned telephone the proportion of households was 4.20 percent among the Chetties and none among the tribes owned telephone. In this context what is more distressing to note is the fact that some of the infrastructure facilities the migrants have been able to develop on the tribal account. To illustrate the State Electricity Board administers a special scheme for the electrification of tribal houses. The scheme is that if the households do the wiring the cost in drawing the line will be met by the department. Whereas in the case of others all the costs have to be borne by the beneficiary. Others particularly the migrants have invented a method by which one of the tribal households get wired either by influencing the tribal department or at the cost of the migrant and makes the application for connection. Thus they are also able to get the electricity connection without extra cost. A number of such cases do exist. In the case of road development too in the name of tribal colony preferential allocation is done though the benefit flow peripherally to the tribes. At the individual household level also the disparity is most conspicuous and had worsened over the years. Migrants were the most successful in exploiting the land resources and reaping the prosperity. At the same time the Chetties and tribes still lag far behind. Concrete evidence to this in terms of differential economic status was given in the preceding chapter. We make a further comment on the disparity and the underlying reasons a little later.

Ecological Costs

Another important deleterious consequence of migration is that in the process of development the entire eco system of the region has come to confront pressure. The thick forests with rich flora and fauna have been transformed into land of human settlements and intensive agriculture. This is not the case just with the particular village we studied but is true of almost all of the large scale settlements of Travancore people in Malabar as most of their settlements were close to the forest area where encroachment was vast open. Invariably on private/ revenue/ reserved forests large-scale encroachment had taken place. The settlers were united and they were able to enlist the political support given their numerical strength and unity. The economic prosperity and their dominance in the socio-economic sphere too aided this process. Thus no matter whether it was encroachment over private land or public land, they came to be indiscriminately protected by the State administration. What happened in Pulpally village we have depicted is well narrative of this. Further to one's dismay what indeed happened in the village was the indiscriminate burning of trees. The settlers were uncertain as to the ownership entitlement of the land in the beginning. Also in the initial years of migration cultivation was not much organised and they had grown short duration crops without much felling of trees. But later vantom destruction followed. For instance lemongrass oil distillation required large-scale firewood and indiscriminately trees were felled and burned. Besides with the introduction of plantation crops as stated by them given the uncertainty to the ownership title over the land they set fire and cleared the forest.

What is more distressing to note is that even now this destruction of forest is taking place in the region at an alarming rate. They now work in tandem with the official machinery. The Church is still in the forefront in many areas to fight for protecting the peasants even illegally. Some of the recent incidents are narrative of this. Vadekkekalam issue of encroachment had its origin as early as 1987. In the year the Thalassery Taluk Land Board in its judgement notified 156 acres of land in the possession of M/s Pothen Joseph and Sons Pvt.Ltd as excess land. When the issue went to the court, the High Court on Oct.21, 1994 directed the Land Board to re-survey the entire land in the possession of the company. On the basis of this re-survey the Land Board on Dec. 1995 declared 1117.25 acres of land as surplus. The original estate spread over 2000 acres is on the hilly terrain. Pothen Joseph of Alapuzha bought it from Puthenveetil Narayani Amma in 1942 when the region was under the Madras Province. The erstwhile Madras Govt. Passed the Madras Preservation of Private Forest Act (M P P F Act) in 1949. In 1951 Pothen Joseph handed over 2082.37 acres to M/s Pothen Joseph and Sons Pvt. Ltd. The land was then re-registered in 1955 on a special sanction of the then Collector as per the provisions of the M P P F Act. Following the enactment of the Kerala Land Reforms Act, Pothen Joseph started selling the land in small pieces to settlers since 1969 apparently to evade the possible declaration of the land as excess land under the K L R Act. The settlers got possession of areas in excess of the extent of lands they bought from Pothen Joseph by encroaching the neighbouring revenue forest. There were several such cases. The High Court had finally ordered eviction of settlers and to take possession of the land. The authorities were also directed to render all assistance to the Tahasildar to evict the settlers from the land before February 23 1998 and to file a compliance report. On a plea of the District Collector and the Tahasildar the Court extended the deadline for eviction till March 15 and to file the compliance report on March 16. The farmers were organised and were fighting for their cause since the problems surfaced. The organisation was known as the Vadakkekalam Karshaka Samrakshana Samithi (Vadakkekalalm Farmers Protection Organisation) an affiliate of the Malabar Karshaka Samithi (M K S, a Church sponsored organisation). The farmers intensified the fight and on the day of reckoning all of them assembled to fight against the eviction. Scores of priests and nuns were placed in the crowd. Further to cite the connection of the Church, a few days earlier to this the Thalassery Archbishop and the Bishop Emeritus Mar. George Valiyamatom and Mar Sebastian Valloppally observed one-day fast demanding government intervention to save the farmers from eviction. The atmosphere was tense on the day of eviction, as the people were ready to face any eventuality. While they sat on the road leading to the estate land in anticipation of the arrival of officials, on the other side there were over 650 police personnel to assist the revenue official's. This continued till the evening of March 15 and in the evening the Tahasildar who has been waiting for the Collector's order from morning got an oral instruction to put off eviction for a few days. Later it is reported that the Kerala Assembly adopted unanimously the Kerala Stay of Eviction Proceedings Bill intended mainly to prevent the eviction of farmers at Vadakkekalam for one year. It is reported that the purpose of the bill was to obtain sufficient time to work out how this problem could be resolved. The government was unable to implement the Court order because if it attempted to evict the farmers it would invite the wrath of the settlers and the Church. On the expiry of the bill the period was extended for another two years. So far no action was taken. The farmers are now planning to resume their agitation, as the extented period is about to expire. How organised and influential the settlers are can well be understood from the above incident.

Forest Mafia has also emerged in the region as a secondary development of migration again giving way for the looting of the forest wealth, mainly timber. Behind this is the timber lobby. They operate with the support of the official machinery. What happened in Peria of Wayanad is well narrative of this. Here trees spread over 139 acres of forestland was looted through fraudulent means in January and February 2000. When news spread that there is large scale felling of trees from the forest the authorities swung into action. Transportation of logs was blocked. 11 officials were suspended from the forest department. Even official estimate, which is conservative, put the total value of trees felled as Rs. 1.2 crore. The modus operandi is like this. The timber Mafia manages to get Mukthiyar (possession certificate) for the patta land (revenue land) adjacent to the forests. Then with the connivance of the revenue and forest-officials the trees are felled from the adjacent forests using the pattayems of the revenue land. This is what happened. The title deeds were given in contravention of the law. An enquiry also revealed serious lapses on the part of the district revenue department and the forest department. These incidents thus give ample testimony to the fact that on a vast scale destruction of forest is going on even now. Behind this are again the migrants.

Another significant ill effect of migration is the degradation of the soil. The soil was earlier noted for its richness. In fact it was the fertility of the soil that attracted many to Pulpally. Before migration the agrarian practices were more environment friendly. While in paddy fields one crop was grown in dry lands it was shifting cultivation. Thus crop intensity was at its minimum and the system had positive consequences for the ecology of the area, its natural resource and environment. Natural fertilizers were also applied a plenty and apart from this natural decomposition of tree leaves significantly added fertility to the soil. Thus whatever crops were grown they were rewarded immensely with high yield. On migration however as evidenced in an earlier chapter there was intensive land use which had its adverse impact on the soil. Loss of vegetative cover meant loss of natural fertilization. Thus over the years they found that the crop yield has gone down substantially and the reason was poor quality of soil. The difference in the yield level of some of the crops, which we have compiled from the respondents, gives an overall idea about this problem. The same is shown in Table 7.2. The figures given in the table are only rough indicators as the yield level in the earlier period was collected out of the memory of the respondents. Also there was no common reference year.

Table 7.2

Difference in the yield of crops

Crops	Yield		
	Beginning	Current	Col 3 as % of Col 2
Padddy (Para per acre)	310.61	195.67	62.99
Yam (Kg. per plant)	8.40	2.87	34.16
Tappioca (Kg. per plant)	13.13	3.76	28.63
Ginger (in gunny bags) per gunny bag of seed)	15.38	7.74	50.32
Turmeric (in gunny bags per gunny bag of seed)	15.91	5.00	31.43
Coffee (quintal per acre)	10.65	6.20	58.22
Pepper (quintal per acre)	14.89	5.45	36.60
Banana (Kg. per plant)	24.57	10.11	41.14

As can be observed from the table in the case of a number of crops such as tapioca, turmeric, elephant yam and pepper the decline in the yield level was perceptible, as the current yield was less by 40 percent. In the case of other crops too there was loss in yield.

Here it may be mentioned that the agricultural promotion policy of the government too has played a significant role in depleting the natural fertility of the soil. Chemical and inorganic manures were subsidized and popularized inducing the farmers to apply them indiscriminately. The same was also done in an unscientific manner as assistance was in kind leaving farmers with no option. This too has played a large role in the destruction of soil fertility. Further it too need to be stated that given the agro-climatic features of the region the cropping pattern they follow and the agricultural practices they undertake now have damaging effect upon the valuable natural resource. Quite significantly long duration crops and plantation crops are gaining more area at the cost of short duration crops. Rubber, areca nut, coconut etc are such plantation crops and most of these crops are introduced recently. In fact even paddy fields were converted into areca nut fields annually at an accelerated rate. The shift is at the cost of short duration crops. Such crops give no rest to land and reduce fertility. Also given the landscape of the village the agricultural practices they follow have adverse consequences on the soil fertility. Crops on hill slopes are highly prone to soil erosion resulting in run off of topsoil during the rain. Tilling further leads to the erosion of the topsoil getting the land degraded as during rainy season they get washed away. Pepper, which is one of the prominent crops, has such practices. Thus the truth is that most of the land has become degraded in the area and the continued sustainability of the agriculture is a big question. There are other contributing factors for this development course to which a mention will be made in one of the following sections.

The landscape of the area too has undergone change. Most of the paddy fields have become coconut, rubber and areca nut farms. Thus at an accelerated rate the paddy fields are shrinking in the village. The rivers and channels, which were a source of irrigation either, have shrinked/ disappeared due to the encroachment on sides by the farmers. In some of the cases 10 to 15 feet wide streams have been reduced to 2 to 3 feet wide streams. Also the sedimentation has affected the water storage capacity of the streams by which irrigation got badly affected. Fish, which was abundant in earlier time and provided nutritious food to the natives, has become totally extinct with this development. The high amount of intense rainfall and slopes makes the area prone to severe soil erosion. Given the agro-climatic conditions intensive cultivation is also not desirable.

Change is also notable in the climatic conditions of the area. While in the old days it used to rain for 9 months with three months of intensive rain now even in the monsoon season rain has become scarce. Thus the agricultural economy has become vulnerable to the vagaries of monsoon. Year after year the climate is becoming warmer. The adaptability of plantation crops like areca nut and coconut bears this fact out. To note, the climate conditions of Wayanad was not suitable for the crops in the old days as they required warm conditions to ripe and they hardly ripped. The situation has changed and they have become adaptable due to the warm conditions and the gain in the area by these crops testifies this. In the case of rubber too there were problems that the latex hardly set out and thus flow continuously. The phenomenon has changed and now many owns rubber plantation in the village.

Also in the earlier days there was abundant water availability in the village and as mentioned even small pits provided water in all seasons. Springs were seen in plenty. But now springs are rare. Ground water is overexploited. Digging of too many wells has brought down the water level. No doubt tube wells have made its appearance and is further aggravating the situation. Side by side there is excessive use of water for short-term gains accelerating the water problem. More important environmental issue is the loss of bio diversity. Several plant varieties including medicinal varieties have become extinct with the indiscriminate felling of trees and clearing of the forest for cultivation. This is also the case with the animals and other living things. To mention big mountain cobra, swan, crab, fox, microorganisms of the soil, etc. have become extinct as listed by them. Crabs were always a threat to the crops. The pesticides applied indiscriminately made them extinct. In an inter connected manner as fox used to eat the crab the fox too got poisoned and as said is extinct now. To sum up an ecological problem is steadily on the rise in the village.

In this context mention may be made about the incidence of tenancy in the village. There are class and type of land specificity to tenancy. Further to note even among the migrants who have migrated with the intention to practice cultivation on their own the leasing out practice is observable. Broadly there are two types of tenancy i.e. share cropping tenancy and tenancy in which the land is made available on rental basis either in cash or kind rent. The leasing practice exists both in the case of wetland and dry land. Wetlands are mainly leased for paddy cultivation. On a very marginal scale banana and elephant yam is also cultivated on leased in wetlands. Where as in the case of dry land, leasing is done mainly for the cultivation of ginger, tapioca and elephant yam. The incidence of leasing in practice among the sample households is shown in Table 7.3. Among the sample households 31 cases of lease in practice was noticed (8.31percent of total households) involving a total area of 45.21 acres (an average area

Table 7.3

Leased in land area (in acres)

Category	Dry land		Wet land		All	
	No.	Area	No.	Area	No.	Area
Migrants	11	36.74	1	0.73	12	37.47
Chetties	3	0.69	4	2.40	7	3.09
Tribals	1	0.25	11	4.40	12	4.65
All	15	37.68	16	7.53	31	45.21

of 1.46 acres). The size of leased in land was highest among the migrants, 3.12 acres on an average by 12 households (6.19 percent). At the same time it was 0.44 acre on an average by 7 Chetty households (7.29 percent). The lowest leased in land was among the Tribes 0.38 acre on an average by 12 tribal households (13.19 percent). Thus the number of households having leased in land was highest among the tribes. Type of land wise interesting observations can be made from the table. Out of 15 leased in dry land cases 11 (73.33

percent) was leased in by the migrants on an average 3.34 acres. In the case of others the leased in area was considerably low less than a quarter of an acre on an average. Thus the migrants mostly leased in dry lands. As opposed to this it can be seen from the table that wetlands are mostly leased in by the tribes. Accordingly out of 16 cases 11 (68.75 percent) were accounted by the tribes. They on an average had leased in 0.40 acre. The practice was also high in the case of Chetty households as there were 4 such cases involving an average area of 0.60 acre. There was only 1 case among the migrants who had taken on lease wetland to the extent of 0.73 acre. Thus the wetlands are mostly leased in by the tribes and the dry lands by the migrants.

Coming to the incidence of leasing out practices again more or less a similar observation can be made (Table 7.4). There were 28 such cases (7.35 percent of the total households) involving a total area of 25.18 acres (0.90 acre on an average by each). The size of leased out land was thus less compared to the size of leased in land among the sample households. The leased out land was more among the native inhabitants as they accounted for 75 percent of such cases. There were 7 such cases

Table 7.4

Land leased out (in acres)

Category	Dry land		Wet land		All	
	No.	Area	No.	Area	No.	Area
Migrants	-	-	7	8.68	7	8.68
Chetties	1	0.50	11	9.79	12	10.29
Tribals	9	6.21	-	-	9	6.21
All	10	6.71	18	18.47	28	25.18

(3.61 percent) among the migrants involving 1.24 acres per migrant. Type of land wise again interesting observations can be made. None of the migrants had leased out the dry land. Among the Chetty households also the incidence was less as only one such case we came across. Where as 9 out of 10 leased out cases of dry land was noticed among the tribes. Further it can be seen that the leasing out of wetland was done by the migrants and Chetties as all the cases were confined to them. None of the tribal category had leased out wetland. Before we make a comment on the reasons for the observed pattern of tenancy let us consider the magnitude of lease in practices for which the net leased in land area is considered. Taking the households as a whole the net leased in area was low as out of 1194.68 acres of owned area the leased in area comes to 20.03 acres or 1.67 percent. At the same time among the various classes distinct pattern is noticeable (Table 7.5). All the net leased in land area of 28.79 acres was among the

Table 7.5

Land leased out (in acres)

Category	Dry land	Wet land	All
Migrants	36.74	-7.95	28.79
Chetties	0.19	-7.39	-7.20
Tribals	-5.96	4.40	-1.56
All	30.97	-10.94	20.03

migrants. At the same time the natives leased out land on a net basis, 7.20 acres by the Chetty households and 1.56 acre by the tribes. Type of land wise the already observed pattern follows clearly. Almost all the dry lands, 99.48 percent of the total was leased in by the migrants and on a net basis 5.96 acres were leased out by the tribes. On the other hand the tribes had leased in on a net basis wetland to the extent of 4.40 acres while the other two classes leased out the wetland.

There are well meaning reasons for the observed pattern of lease practices. While paddy cultivation in the state in general has become uneconomic it is particularly so in villages like this. It is a more labour intensive crop and as widely known labour cost has gone up substantially. At the same time the market price of paddy turned out to be unremunerative. Further the fertility of the soil has diminished and irrigation prospects are also on the decline with the disappearance of the channels and due to water shortage. All this has come to make an impact upon the yield level of paddy and its prospects. One of the Chetties have put the case more perceptively that with wet land paddy cultivation they have become poor where as with dry land farming the migrants have become rich. Thus the tendency on the part of the migrants and to some extent Chetties is to give up paddy cultivation. The tribes have unemployed labour and as a strategy to cope up with the distress situation even if uneconomical they are taking the land on lease. The landowner provides material inputs. Harvest is shared sometimes equally including the hay.

Here it may be highlighted that even paddy fields are kept fallow. The magnitude of the problem can be deduced from Table 7.6 in which the incidence and size of fallow land on wet area is given. There were 28 cases where paddy fields are kept fallow to the extent of 21.73 acres (0.77 acre on an average). Out of 28 cases 17 (60.71 percent) were migrants and they accounted for 51.86 percent of the total area kept fallow followed by the Chetties who accounted for 35.71 percent of cases

Table 7.6

Incidence of fallow paddy land (in acres)

Category	No	Area	Av. Area
Migrants	17	11.27	0.66
Chetties	10	9.46	0.95
Tribals	1	1.00	1.00
All	28	21.73	0.77

and 43.53 percent of area. Evidently the incidence was very low among the tribes. At the same time dry land farming in the area is more profitable and this consideration led the migrants in particular to lease in such land. Apart from the less enterprising nature of tribes compared to migrants they have resource constraints in planning and developing the dry land. The plantation crops, which require timely farm maintenance, the tribes are not able to do as they mainly depend upon wage labour. Thus dry lands are leased out by a number of them.

Political and Social Impact

There were few notable side effects on the social and political front too. Let us now make a brief comment on them.

The Naxalbari Movement

There were ill effects of migration on the political and social life of the people. On the political front as mentioned above there was the emergence of revolutionary organisation called the Naxalbari movement. This put the village on the map of political movement of the country. However as far as the village is concerned the overall impact was mixed as on the one hand the event brought misery to the people and on the other hand paved the way for the governmental initiative for the development of the village. A brief mention to the circumstances in which the movement originated, its actions and its overall impact are most appropriate to note here.

Historical events reveal that certain movements originate out of a propitious environment. In the case of the emergence of the naxalbari movement in the village this was almost true. One of the important factors was the forced eviction of the encroachers from the temple land. The hardships of the migrants were documented already. The police and the temple guards deployed to protect the land adopted inhuman methods running on the lines of setting fire to houses, destruction of agricultural crops, looting of valuables etc. Some of them said that there was also sexual harassment of women. All this was at its climax when Sub-inspector Allappan was in charge. It was also said that he forced many to sign fake documents, threatened the people and extracted money. Several migrants are charged in fake cases. Thus deep wounds were inflicted in the minds of the migrant community. It is said that even a passion to kill Allappan developed in the mind some of the activists. The then prevailing agrarian relation was another contributing factor. The system was equivalent to slavery as far as the relationship between the tribes and the Chetties were concerned. Tribes were is dire poverty while granaries of the chetties bulged with stocks of paddy. Many migrants were the sympathisers of the Communist party. They considered themselves as working class and Communists were the saviors of the working class. The one who pioneered the idea in the village was Etoor Joseph. In the beginning he conducted processions singly propagating the communist ideas. He practiced the ideology too. The 5 acres of land he purchased was distributed to 25 persons. Another one who was active in the beginning was Kissan Thomas. It was also around this time that there was the split in the Communist party. Further the naxalbaris were striking at few places. The one incident, which influenced the followers, was the armed revolution by the farmers in Andhra Pradesh village called Naxalbari. This even earned the praise of the Communist party of China. Around this time the Naxal movement was making its appearance in several parts of the State too. Some of the prominent leaders were based in Kozhikode. The situation in Pulpally was also deteriorating day by day. It was also in this context that disillusioned with the division in the Communist party that a number of people left the Communist party and they were attracted by the revolutionary movement. Many in Pulpally followed suit. The above-mentioned persons were in the forefront as leaders. Their intention was to launch Guerilla war. The condition of the village was very suitable to their activities. There was neither transport nor communication facilities. It was cut off from the main land with forests on the three sides. In the meanwhile attempts were made to organize the scheduled tribes by Kissan Thomas. Thus a number of people were mobilized within the village and study camps were organized. An idea struck the mind of Thomas and that was to throw a challenge before the state leaders. Thus he wrote to the state leaders stating that Pulpally is the ideal place for them to strike, as the conditions were well appropriate. The leaders also took the challenge in the right spirit. Thus the local organizers came in contact with the then state leaders such as Kunnikal

Narayanan, Mandakini, Ajitha and Varghese. Study camps were organized, people were mobilized and plan was also evolved. The initial intention was to attack some of the police stations including Pulpally and to mobilize arms and ammunitions for the fight. Another agenda was to conduct a public trial of Sub Inspector Allappan and to give a fitting punishment. Some weapons were mobilized for the initial strike. First it was planned to attack the Thalassery police station and a group was deputed for the task. After the strike they were to join the rest at Thirunelli. For the same the route through the forest was marked. November 20,1968 was the date fixed for the action. Thus a team of 1000 persons through different routes reached Thalassery. But they could not strike on the day fixed. Many started departing. On the third day i.e.Nov.23 the police station was attacked. The operation was a failure as most of the members ran away. A number of them were arrested later. Radio news came that about 600 persons attacked the Thalassery police station and no one was arrested. The news encouraged the Pulpally gang. Till then the Pulpally gang spent their time in the forest reading the Mao literature and undergoing training. Finally on Nov 24th early morning the Pulpally station was attacked by a group of about 60 persons. They were armed with rifles, dynamites etc. On reaching near the camp one of the dynamites accidentally bursted leading to the loss of one arm of one of the participants. This alerted the police and they fired the mob. When the mob returned fire seeing the size of the mob the police ran away. The targeted sub-inspector Allappan was out of station. One of the havildar Kunhi Krishnan Nair was beaten to death though it was not planned. Another one succumbed to injuries in the hospital. One of them put an idea that as a mark of their success Ajitha's handmark be put on the wall of the police camp with blood. Thus with the blood of the dead havildar the imprint was made. Later Ajitha said that to tarnish the image of the naxals the hand imprint was done by the police with the hand of the diseased police constable. However a participant in the attack testified to us that it was done with the hand of Ajitha. They could not mobilize as many weapons as they expected. All of them after the operation marched to Chekadi, one of the oldest settlements of the chetties. Two houses of chetties were attacked and they took possession of one rifle, gold, cash, paddy and utensils. Though one of the Chetty was shot he survived. The paddy and utensils collected was distributed to the tribes. After this they moved to the forest. Accidentally again one of the dynamites bursted in the forest and Kissan Thomas was seriously injured. As no medical help could be rushed he turned out to be a liability to others. Thus he was shot dead at his will by one of the comrades. Then they moved to Thirunelli. It was proposed to meet both the Thalassery and Pulpally gangs at Thirunelli. For weeks together they camped in the forest. As the Thalassery gang failed to turn up all of them got impatient. On Dec.26 after more than one month they decided to disburse. Most of them moved towards the Thalassery route through the demarked forest area. At a place called Atakkathodu the people noticed Ajitha and the group. Some of them went to the Church and rang the bell to alert the people. The people assembled, caught them and handed over to the police.

The incident received publicity all over the country and Pulpally became notorious as a land of Naxals. It was also a blessing in disguise as a number of development works got initiated. A police station was established at Pulpally. Communication facilities got a big boost. Road was constructed and the main route was developed for the visit of the Governor. All of them were of the opinion that naxal movement has contributed for the development of Pulpally especially for the infrastructure development. At the same time it is also a fact that the people of the village were subjected to several hardships consequent upon the event. Police atrocities were at its climax particularly on the Communist workers and activists of the Karshaka Sangom (farmers organization). Incidentally a meeting held in Pulpally led the authorities to believe the connection of the Sangom. Thus on 22nd November two days before the incident to protest against the eviction the Sangam convened a big meeting in Pulpally town. The speeches were provocative as the people were advised to fight. The police connected the two events. Several leaders were taken to the Police camp and brutally beaten up. A number of them went underground. To teach the enemies a lesson the influential made use of the opportunity. Thus the enemies were branded as naxals and subjected to police harassment. Pulpally people in general came to be branded as extremists by the outsiders. When went out even hotel accommodation were denied to the people if recognized as from Pulpally. Bus travel too became difficult. A situation emerged that the people have to procure a certificate from the village officer as not a naxalite.

Even arranging marriage alliance with outsiders became difficult. It was also rumored that people were leaving Pulpally after the naxalite attack. This encouraged many to migrate as land were expected at a cheap rate.

Here it may also be mentioned that one and a half years back at the instance of the High Court a fresh investigation into a case connected to this incident is being ordered. It was the death of Varghese who was the brain behind the entire incident. After disbursing from the forest he concentrated in Thirunelli, one of the other backward villages of Wayanad. There again he fought against the social evils of tribal exploitation and other agrarian evil practices. In fact during the course of our visit to the place we came to notice that there was widespread appreciation among many about his work in the area. However the police caught him in 1971 and murdered. At the time it was touted as an encounter death. According to this version when the police went inside the forest in search of the Naxalite leader, the police team was fired upon and Varghese lost his life in the ensuing encounter. However after almost three decades one of the retired police constables came out with a story that he shot dead the unarmed Varghese as per the order of the superior officer. He made the disclosure following a pang of conscience. His revelation made a controversy and demand for a fresh investigation into the murder was raised by several human rights organisations. One of them approached the Court seeking an investigation by the Central Bureau of Investigation. The police constable also filed an affidavit before the High Court admitting that he had killed Varghese at the instance of the superior officer. The Court has directed the C B I to probe the case and the investigation is in progress.

Tribal Land Alienation

History is replete with the problem of deprivation meted out by the tribes. The problem of land alienation is the most important of all. This is an also an age-old problem. Protective legislation goes far back to the British period. The earliest law date back to 1839 when the British administration enacted legislation concerning the separation of agency areas from other areas. In 1917 the law known as the Agency Tract Interest and Land Transfer Act was introduced with a view to protect the land of tribes and regulating the rates of interest in the Madras Presidency. Section 4 of the Act laid down that not withstanding any rule of law or enactment to the contrary, any transfer of immovable property situated in the agency tracts by a member of the hill tribe shall be absolutely null and void unless made in favour of another member of a hill tribe, or with the previous consent in writing of the agent or any other Presiding Officer. In 1935 the Govt. of India passed an Act giving more powers to the Governor in the governance of the scheduled areas. Independent India further articulated this as the Directive Principles of the Indian Constitution laid down that "the state shall promote with special care the educational and economic interests of the weaker sections of the people, and in particular of the scheduled castes and the scheduled tribes, and shall protect them from social injustice and ill forms of exploitation". Also in recognition of the gravity of the problem of land alienation the central government evolved a directive to regulate the encroachment on forestland and this promises the adivasis (tribes) to give title to land that they have cultivated for decades. To qualify for this it has been stipulated that they must prove that their encroachment happened before Oct. 1980 and that their legal land holdings do not exceed two hectares.

Despite all the protective legislation the fact is that tribes got alienated form their land en mass. According to the 29th Report of the Commissioner of Scheduled Castes and Scheduled Tribes till 1990, 40 percent of the adivasi had been displaced from their own habitat.

In Kerala the issue has become all the more serious in recent years. The problem is closely associated with the migration we study. Though this was going on for a long time in the last three decades the issue has become controversial. To elaborate in brief, taking into account the gravity of the problem in 1975 the Kerala Scheduled Tribe (Regulation on Transfer of Lands) and Restriction of Alienated Lands Act was passed unanimously by the State Legislature. However the Bill came into effect in 1982. The bill declared that all transactions of the adivasi lands during the period 1962-82 had become invalid and the land should be given back to the original owners. All the land transfers from the adivasis to the non-adivasis were restricted from 1982 onwards. The Act of 1975 was included in the Ninth Schedule so that the law should not be challenged in the Court. Though the Act was passed the regulations for the restoration was evolved on Oct '8th 1986 and as per the regulations all the land transactions effected from 1962 to 1986 were made invalid. When the proceedings for the restorations were initiated stiff organized resistance came from the settlers. In 1988 the matter became much more controversial. One Dr Nalla Thampi of Sultan Battery filed a writ in the High Court. The Judge accepting the writ, send notices to the authorities to report the reason for the delay in the execution of the Bill and demanding action as per the Acts. There was lukewarm response from the government. A petition was again filed. On this basis on Jan 21, 1991 the Justice issued an order to produce the action taken report. As per the report submitted it is said that in the state 8754 applications have been received for restoration covering an area of 9909.45 ha. Out of this 463 cases have been solved and 544.56 ha. have been restored. In 1993 the High Court on the petition ordered for the restoration of all the alienated land to the tribes. The state government pleaded that the tribes have no financial position to pay compensation for restoration. In 1996 Sept. 13 the High Court again interfered and stipulated that the land which need not involve compensation be restored without any appeal. Six months time was granted. The full bench later endorsed this order of the division bench. In the meanwhile the government initiated measures for the revision of the Act. Thus on March 9, 1999 the government brought a new Adivasi Land Act (Restriction of Transfer by Restoration of the Land to the ST's Act). It was proposed that all the landless tribes would be given one-acre substitute land. It was also decided that those who are having below 2 ha. of adivasi land be exempted from the Act and their land need not be taken away. The Act too was challenged in the Court. The bill too was a non-starter as far as the restoration or provision of substitute land is concerned. On the one side the settlers are not prepared to give up any piece of land and is determined to fight it out by any means. On the other side the tribes are also now a days organized and demanding the restoration of the same land. The effort of the state in issuing substitute land was also not successful as the tribes had objected as the land were hardly cultivable.

Tribes account for a significant proportion in the demographic composition of Wayanad. The size of migration too was more in the district. No surprise the problem of land alienation is much more serious in the district. In the district as on 30th Sept. 1999 there were

2279 cases involving an area of 3793.22 acres. Thus in terms of numbers the share of the district comes to 26.03 percent and in terms of area 15.50 percent (when compared with the back dated state level figures presented above). Out of 2279 cases 1806 cases were decided in favour of the tribes covering an area of 2718.14 acres. The period wise number of cases shown in Table 7.7 reveals that a significant number of cases involving 52.43 percent of area occurred in the post 1975 period.

Table 7.7

Period wise distribution of land alienation

Period	No. of cases	Percentage	Area (acres)	Percentage
1960 -75	419	23.20	1036.09	47.57
1975- 82	697	38.59	721.33	33.12
1982-86	538	29.79	358.04	16.44
1986-96	152	8.42	62.68	2.88
Total	**1806**	**100.00**	**2178.14**	**100.00**

Source: Complied from the records of the Office of the Asstt. Collector, Manantavady.

Even during the 1986-96 period there occurred tribal land alienation. The size distribution of 1806 cases shown in Table 7.8 reveals that a number of cases involved large area. Thus while nearly two fifth of the cases involved up to half an acre, another 22.54 percent involved between 0.51-1 acre and another 15.45 percent between 1.01- 2 acres. Out of the total, 14.56 percent of cases involved above 3 acres. While this is one side of the problem the other is the implementation part. Thus the official data revealed that out of 1806 cases only 68 cases involving an area of 36.19 acres were given possession

Table 7.8

Distribution of tribal land alienation cases by size of land

Size class (acres)	No. of cases	Percentage
Less than 0.50	710	39.31
0.50-1.00	407	22.54
1.01- 2.00	279	15.45
2.01-3.00	147	8.14
3.01-4.00	126	6.98
4.01-5.00	66	3.65
5.01-6.00	48	2.66
6.01 and above	23	1.27
All	1806	100.00

going by the official records. Out of this dismally in 2 cases actual physical restoration was done. In the case of others actual restoration was found as impossible due to strong physical resistance of the settlers. Thus for all practical purposes it can be said that so far no progress was made in restoring the alienated land to the tribes in the district. The problem was much more alarming as there are significant number of unreported cases since the tribes hardly come forward to assert their rights. The evidence that has to be produced by the tribes to claim restoration was reportedly not available. Coming specifically to the village, official records indicated that there were 42 such cases involving an area of 5.856 ha. None of them has been restored so far.

From the field observations we have been able to learn that the migrants adopted a variety of strategies to grab the land. Giving advances either in cash or in kind (in the form of paddy and tapioca) in instalments and accounting them without the knowledge of the borrower was one such method. In this case on the one hand the amount of credit got inflated and on the other hand an exorbitant interest was charged rendering it difficult for the debtor to get extricated from the liability. Ultimately the migrants took possession of the land. Here again in many cases they used to attach more than the land they agreed to. Thus cheating at the time of measurement happened with the support of the surveyor. On liquor account too land grab happened. Another important method was through share cropping arrangements. Thus the migrants lease in land from the tribes and ultimately claim over the land is established. Pure encroachment was another strategy. While in certain cases when land is situated adjacent to that of the migrant gradual encroachment occurred and in the case of others encroachment used to be all of a sudden. We have been able to learn that even when notice of restoration was served the straightforward attitude of the people made them not to pursue the case on sentimental ground that their deceased parents borrowed the money. Here it need to be said that a significant number of Chetties too were victims and lost land. A case is well illustrative of the nature of fraudulent practices adopted by the migrants. A Chetty used to drink and play cards in the company of the migrants. In the process he got indebted to the extent of Rs. 4000 to a Christian migrant. To settle the same an oral agreement was reached and that was to sell him 0.20-acre land. Later under the influence of liquor the agreement was recorded showing a debt of Rs. 40000 carrying 100 percent interest. When the migrant came to claim the amount there was dispute. Finally at the instance of some mediators he was forced to depart with 1.25-acre land. If this was the experience of the Chetties as to the nature and dimension of exploitation of the tribes the less said the better.

Unwed Mothers

If on the economic front land alienation is the most serious problem of the tribes on the social front it is sexual abuse and the problem of unwed mothers. By and large this can also be said as a migration associated social problem. Though isolated cases are observable in several of the villages the problem has assumed to an alarming proportion in Thirunelli and Thrisselery area belonging to the Manantavady taluk of Wayanad district. In one of the wards in the village we have conducted an extensive discussion with a cross section of people to get an insight into the various facets of this social problem. We were also able to have a very brief discussion with a few unwed mothers with the help of the local social workers. Some of our observations are quite startling and run contrary to the common perception about the problem.

On the incidence we have been able to note that there were about 62 unwed mothers in the ward. All of them were tribal women. The first case as recollected by an informant happened in 1952. Some of the cases had a chain effect and the extreme case was that the daughter and the grand daughter of one of the unwed mothers happened to be unwed mother. The one case, which came to our notice in the Pulpally village was also identical as the daughter of an unwed mother turned out to be an unwed mother. Out of 62 cases 22 unwed mothers later got married and the rest continues as unwed. Except one all others were wed to tribal men.

Some of the other features are quite revealing. Most of the cases are identifiable among the Paniya and Adiya denominations of the tribes. Behind this sexual exploitation of the tribes were the non-tribes cutting across religion/caste. The list includes those who migrated permanently and those temporarily camped in the village in connection with temporary works, criminals who came to hide in the place, bus transport employees camping in the area, police personnel etc. The man behind each case is an open secret. Though cases were recurring over the years only recently the problem came to be known to the outside world. In a number of cases the relation is regularly maintained and as aptly put by the social worker of the area they are unwed mothers in the daytime and they lead a wedded life in the night. Multiple children of unwed mothers born out of same person hints at this fact. In a number of cases men have formally wed wife and still they continue with this illegal relation. In certain cases the person is sometimes compelled by the unwed wife to visit the formally wed wife. Quite interestingly even financial help flows to the males from some of the unwed mothers. At the same time there are unwed mothers who gave birth to multiple children of different persons. For instance the unwed mother 'A' had one child born out of a high caste youth 'X'. He openly admits it and provided for her maintenance. He was also notorious for this activity and when in another case he was falsely implicated and put in jail 'A' again become pregnant and gave birth to a child purportedly of another person. 'X' disowned her and subsequently she again gave birth to two children of different persons. Though 'X' is prepared to look after his child she is not prepared to depart with the child. Though a number of cases have been booked and legal actions were initiated except one or two cases all the other cases got compromised. Only one case is now referred for the DNA test. Even in this case the father of the girl who is a watchman in the Forest Department as understood by us is being harassed for not falling in line.

Before examining the root cause for the occurrence of this social problem let us pause for a moment to examine the social set up of the village as it has a bearing on this problem. The area witnessed extreme form of landlordism. As per the prevalent practice the tribal communities were more or less slaves and the women were the objects for the sexual enjoyment of the landlords. There was a saying that Mannum Pennum Thambrande (the soil and the girl belong to the landlord). The usual practice was that the males are deputed as watch and ward for the standing crops in the night. Thus the landlords are free to have sex with the tribal women in the night. Understandably there is the permissive sanction of the husband. It is even said that after the marriage the bride has to be kept in the custody of the landlord for the first seven days. No surprise though the fatherhood of the children is open to doubt they were treated as their own by the husband. Being slaves the provision for the living of the entire family came from the landlord. This situation changed. The landlordism came to an end and no longer they are open to this form of sexual abuse. At the same time it has to be admitted that there is still a hangover of the loose moral culture among them and the present day problem is only a variant of the above practice. Apart from this in accordance with our understanding we are to state that there is an enabling environment for this social problem to crop up. One is the prevailing social and economic backwardness of the area and the people.

Poverty is widespread. Employment is seasonal being fully depended upon the agriculture. Educationally it is one of the most backward areas. Suffice it to state pupil have to travel 28 kms. to reach the nearest upper primary school. Thus at a very tender age they are in a nothing doing syndrome. In this situation constant interaction takes place between both sexes. Many times it happens to be in the surroundings of the houses or near the countryside shops. Shop owners are promoting this as a strategy to boost sales. Besides at the time of farm operations males go around the fields and chat with them. Contributing to this was the poverty conditions. In times of distress help in money or in kind flow to the tribal girls. It is also a peculiarity that the tribes are amenable to anything. Above all this is the break up of the traditional system. The Mooppan (leader) of the tribes have become powerless. He can also be easily influenced now with a bottle of liquor. Further it can be said that there is social sanction for the practice among the communities more prone to this. The ritual is called Thappum Pizhayum (penalty) and is performed in the month of metam (April). On the day the girl has to climb the hill and on her return to the village she is absolved of the sin. Further in the contemporary era women have come to play a decisive role in the household affairs. Men have become lazy and alcoholics and being depended upon women they have no voice. Thus women shoulder all the household responsibilities. Disharmony and indiscipline is the order of the day in the households. No surprise in the scenario depicted above there exists fertile ground for the illicit relation to develop.

What is also significant to note in this context is the fact that now the issue has got a much more pervasive face. The politicians and the Mafia groups have come to capitalize from the issue. To say it is equivalent to hitting the dead. This was also the reason why the news spread outside the region all of a sudden though the problem existed in the area for decades. To elaborate, the news came out in 1984. A tribal girl employed for outside work in a house developed an illicit relation with a young member of the house. She became an unwed mother. The man was a congress party worker. The Marxist party seized the opportunity to tarnish the image of the congress. They influenced the mother of the girl and insisted to get him married with the girl. Ultimately a compromise was struck. After this incident the politicians and the Mafia groups have started exploiting the situation. Accordingly we have been able to learn that left to themselves the tribes used to suppress the incident and accepts the outcome silently. Now once noticed the outside elements become active and instigate the victims. Thus compromise is reached at their instance (usually an amount as compensation is negotiated) and out of the compensation amount a small fraction is only paid to the victims. The middleman appropriates the rest. It is again because of the intervention of these anti-socials that some of the cases got compromised at an advanced stage of legal action. Some of them are so clever and show no hesitation to falsely implicate the innocent. A case can be cited. The person 'X' about whom we have referred above was notorious for this activity in the area. He some how manage to strike compromise every time. When a fresh incident occurred in the locality a group of persons influenced the tribal girl and her parents and accused the person 'X' falsely on the expectation that he will manage the issue. By the time due to his pervasive life he lost most of his wealth. He was also determined not to fight the case. 'X' was jailed for months together. Finally at the instance of his wife the petitioner confessed before the Court about the innocence of 'X' and thereafter he was released. Similar cases do exist. Needless to state in all the deals money gets appropriated by the middleman. Even the police personnel have come to exploit the situation. The victims are sometimes asked to sign some papers often manipulated as either the complaint as revoked or compromised. For the deal huge sums are paid to the police. Further we are told that it was under the influence of Mafia operating in the area that some of the police persons who were on duty in the area got illicit relation and became controversial. Few incidents happened as well intentioned. A police station came up in the village consequent upon the emergence of the naxal movement. Now calm prevails and hence the police is idle. Some of them were induced to cultivation on rented land for which the agents do all the arrangements. In the process in the field they get in touch with the tribal girls and some of them became unwed mothers. To save the face the person managed to get a transfer of course striking a compromise and this is done at the cost of harvest. The agent finally reaps the harvest. But the basic fact remains that the tribal women even in such a distress situation gets exploited.

The incident has brought ill reputation to all the other communities of the area. It is said that as if to a sex heaven people come as tourists for sexual enjoyment. Marriage alliances have become difficult to strike with the people of other villages due to this ill reputation. Further when females go out to neighbouring places once they are sensed as from Thirunelli the behaviour of others suddenly changes as if they are available for sex trafficking. Thus the issue has become a social problem of the entire population of the area.

Communal Problem

The population composition of the village consequent upon migration underwent change leading to an admixture of various communities. To a certain extent communal harmony was also maintained and this was one of the shining features as far as this migration is concerned. At the same time there was an incident which had a communal colour and which had sown the seeds of distrust among the people. This occurred over the ownership right of a piece of land and the issue was also between the migrant groups in the forefront. As we have observed at the initiative of the people fairly good facilities for school education developed in the village. Establishment of a college however remained as an unfulfilled dream for a long time though some attempts were made on this line. A turning point came when the Pulpally temple manager agreed to donate 26 acres of land very close to the town to establish a college. A Trust known as Pashassi Raja Educational Society was formed by the social activists. In the forefront were the migrants. At this juncture a person with the support of the local Sree Narayana Dharma Paripalana Yogam (SNDP is on organisation of ezhava community belonging to the other backward communities in the state) came to claim the right over the land. There was another story. Much earlier to this a Trustee of the temple in writing gave 26 acres of land to four persons belonging to Thalassery without clearly defining the boundaries. It remained as an open land for a long time and later they were unable to locate the land. There was no land tax remittance on their account. As encroachment over the temple land took place this land too can be presumed as encroached. The only land then in the possession of the temple was adjacent to the temple, a prime location. The said owners of the land being based in Thalassery it was difficult for them to stake the claim over the land. Sensing this the person (a migrant about whom we referred above) got the right transferred in his name. He was a prominent member of SNDP. As an organisational support was necessary to establish his right an agreement was reached with the SNDP that the person will fell the trees and the land will be handed over to the SNDP. By the time the relationship between the manager of the temple and the particular Trustee soared. It was in this background to nullify the action of the Trustee the manager came forward to donate the land to the educational society. In effect on the one side the person with the support of the SNDP and on the other side the temple manager with the support of the educational society came to claim the right over the land. When the person constructed a shed it was demolished by the society. Again the SNDP planned to install an idol of Sree Narayana Guru and a day was fixed. The state president of the Yogam was to come for the function. People in general were agitated over the issue and as tension mounted the president was prevented on the way by the Police. Later with the support of the administration the Yogam laid the foundation stone for the statue and in protest against this the educational society organized a mass procession to the disputed site. This led to violence and police firing. It was said that for the first time in the history of the state 50 rounds were fired and in the firing 3 persons died. This happened on July 6th, 1983. In the following two days life was paralysed in the village as bundh was observed. For about a week the village was in the grip of fear as there was high handedness on the part of the police. Associated with this event a police jeep was set fire. This occurred on the bundh day when some of the school children unaware of the bundh were returning from school. They were asked by the Police to remove a roadblock. When the children refused they were beaten and this ignited the feelings of the people and they stoned the police and set fire to the jeep. Ultimately the person was able to get the title over the land and it is widely believed that the administration has gone out of its way to issue title deed under the influence of the Yogam. Thereafter though the dispute went up to the Supreme Court the temple authorities lost the case. The person felled all the trees and handed over the land to the Yogam. The Yogam now owns the land. It is said that the temple authorities were not able to follow up the case in time as one of the suit clerks in the devaswom office played second fiddle to the yogam and suppressed many facts and Court summons. Though the incident was serious in nature it has not led to any permanent disharmony and fight among the communities. Still it cannot be denied that the incident lingers in the memory of many in the village as a black mark. To state, having lost the case the educational society later purchased a piece of land and established the college.

Other Problems

This migration has created other ill effects too. Let us make a brief note on some of them.

Firstly discord and dislike between the natives and the migrants can be said as on the rise. This is a later development. Even when there was encroachment by the migrants and consequent social problems there was harmonious existence between the various communities. In fact the native Chetties extended helping hand to many migrants in times of distress in the beginning. However the subsequent developments within the village made a sharp economic divide between the two communities i.e. the migrants and the locals in general. While the migrants in general and the Christians in particular became more economically successful the natives by and large got sidelined. As noted above the new comers cornered most of the benefits of development and the natives were passive spectators. On the social, cultural and other spheres too they have come to dominate and thus a sense of identity loss and powerlessness has come to be felt by the locals. In our discussion with the Chetties this was fully reflective. To state a few of their remarks: they have (the migrants) become rich, they are clever, we are fools, they now rule, they know how to live and even tribes fail to recognize us. The Chetties also hold a strong feeling that the temple authorities have favoured the migrants. On some other counts also deep wounds are created upon some of the natives. By hook or nook a number of migrants had grabbed the land of the natives including the Chetties. Some of them were cheated financially also. The dispossession was more among the tribes. This feeling gets amplified now as daily they witness the prosperous life of the migrants. It is also a fact that behind the prosperity of the migrants was the hard labour of the tribal labour. They were subjected to exploitation also. This is hardly acknowledged now as even in times of distress no help is provided to the tribes. No surprise the tribes has started expressing it openly and there is displeasure among the migrants.

Clashes too occurs. An incident is narrative of this. Right from the afternoon till late night it is usual for the tribes to gather around the liquor shop in the town, drink and scold the migrants sometimes by naming them. It became intolerable to the migrants. They on their part planned to give a fitting punishment to them. Thus as planned a group of migrants cut off the power supply of the town in the night and manhandled the tribes. While this is one dimension the other is the communal divide. This too is a recent development. The people have started organizing on communal lines. Accordingly the Christians and Hindus of all denominations have their own organizations in the village. This is cutting across the native or migrant consideration. Startilingly community considerations have come to be reckoned above political affiliation in the voting behaviour of the people. Openly elections are fought on communal lines. To some extent we have been able to learn that the Christians who are dominating have started posing challenges to others though not openly.

Production and consumption has become market based and this is a significant post migration development. Commercialization of agriculture, cash economy and dependence on the market for day to day living are the various facets of this development. As a result of this development certain sections have become disadvantaged on account of the market. This may be elaborated in some detail. Introduction of new crops and new cultivation practices led to the profound growth of the agricultural sector in terms of production and productivity. This has led to economic prosperity and generated secondary effect of migration. Precisely rising income meant growing demand for a variety of goods and services of the consumption type, input demand for agriculture, transport and entertainment etc. This in turn has made the economy somewhat diversified. On a closer look it can be seen that the various communities shared the benefits of this development disproportionately. There are various means through which these benefits can be reaped. One is by developing the own farm and here as we outlined the migrants cornered most of the prosperity. Our data not presented here clearly indicated that among the migrants it was the Christians who were able to reap the best out of the development. Undoubtedly the benefit has accrued to the Chetties. However when it comes to other benefits their participation was less. Adoption of openings unleashed by the diversification process specifically adoption of trade, transport, commerce etc. in the village is another way to reap the prosperity. Here the new opportunities that opened up as a result of all this was more or less captured by the migrants in general and the Christians in particular. Some idea about this has been gained from an examination of the nature of diversification of employment discussed in an earlier chapter. To further focus on this aspect let us now consider the religious distribution of the owners of trading/commerce establishments of Pulpally. The same is shown in Table 7.9. As can be learnt from the table 46.15 percent of the trade, business and other establishments were owned by the Christian community and another 35.38 percent by the Hindus and the balance 18.46 percent by the Muslims. Out of Hindus we noted that most of them were the migrants. Thus the domination of the migrants in these activities becomes quite clear. Benefits can also be reaped by the offer of factor services. Here the most important factor is the labour and to the tribes this was the only available factor. No doubt there are

Table 7.9

Religious distribution of the owners of trade/ commerce establishments

Religion	Number	Percentage
Christians	180	46.15
Hindus	138	35.38
Muslims	72	18.46
All	390	100.00

some spillover of benefits to the labour class in the form of rising wages. But being open to market process and the market functionaries known for the exploitation the net benefit they reaped can be said as only either negative or only marginal in size. In tune with this went our observation that there is a widespread perception among the tribes that though the wage rate has increased they are inadequate to sustain them and that their condition has worsened compared to the pre-migration period.

The agricultural economy of the region is in a state of crisis and it is a question of its long run sustainability. There are several reasons to this. As mentioned above the environmental degradation caused by the over exploitation of the land resource has led to a situation of falling agricultural productivity. Monsoon has become irregular impacting on the agricultural prospects. The ground water availability is day by day on the decline badly affecting the agriculture prospects and the life of the people. Agricultural product prices are either stagnant or declining. Coming to the cost of production apart from rising material input cost wage is sizably on the rise. Labour scarcity is also felt in seasons. Apart from the rising wage the labour effort as pointed out by them have gone down again leading to rising labour cost. The impact of all this is that on the one hand more labour saving crops are being substituted and on the other hand proper farm maintenance is not done. Thus again agricultural productivity is on the decline. The practice of keeping fallow the wetland has to be viewed from this angle. The net result of all this is that economic prosperity, which the farmers witnessed has become more elusive in the emerging situation. Most of the farmers are now less prepared to undertake risk and as said by all of them the borrowings for agricultural investment are an unsound proposition. Thus fresh borrowings are less. These facts highlights that the agricultural economy of the region is in crisis. This has further implications. The agricultural prosperity they realized in the earlier years led to the adoption of a high living standard. Also to state some of them have lived beyond the means and in the emerging situation many are finding it difficult to sustain the living standard. Thus new adjustment mechanisms to absorb the shocks are being evolved now by some of them. Thus search for new pastures is now a days taking place on the part of many migrants. The shift is again to less inhabited and underdeveloped lands mainly in Karnataka. While on disposal of land at the present place they can realize a remunerative price in the new place fertile virgin land is available at a cheap rate thus in a way replaying the history of this migration. There are two types of people who adopts this course. One is the upper strata who find it difficult to sustain the high living standard. The other is by the poor sections of the earlier migrants to improve their lot. While permanent shifting is one dimension the other is the seasonal shift to exploit the virgin land. Thus there are enterprising farmers who are taking uncultivated and forestland on lease in seasons mainly for ginger cultivation. Thus forests are cleared and after land development the crops are sown. Labour, mainly tribal labour is transported from the area in groups, as they are familiar with the cultivation practices. As we learnt a number of them were able to reap large prosperity in the beginning for the reason that forest like land was sometimes made available free and on such land they are able to reap good harvest. Implicit in this deal is the benefit of land development to the landowner. Of late however an unhealthy competition is also taking place and some of them are getting exploited in the host land. Accordingly some of them charges heavy rent for the land. So also sometimes the farmers are taken for a ride as harvesting is denied in the pretext of one reason or other by the landowner. Such problems are said as on the rise year after year.

Another distressing phenomenon is the attitudinal change of the people. Of late there is individualism of the pervasive type among the people. This is again a recent development. As acknowledged by all of them the co-operative spirit and collective action has gone a long way in the development of the village. In this not only material but physical effort were pooled no matter whether it was for the development of roads, schools, Church and even private property. Accordingly when they were in distress there was co-operation and as said by one of them all shared one's sorrow. Dismally now this became a thing of the past. Today no one is dependent on the other. There is considerable affluence. This status improvement made them highly individualistic. Further there was the influence of the electronic media too in developing such an attitude.

They also identified the reason and that was status improvement and new material conditions of life. Here again as put by one of them prosperity has become a curse, as no longer there is social life. Such feelings are more among the old. Further as cited by another one even if there was misery there was peace and tranquility to the mind in the past. This is badly missing today. With prosperity people has become egoistic too.

Apart from land alienation the tribes are getting more and more exploited on other accounts too and their condition is getting worsened. This may be elaborated in some detail. The pre-migration social structure was one in which though they were dependent there were customary rights and responsibilities. There was some amount of social security as in times of distress they can fall upon the cultivators. With migration the system underwent change. As already outlined a marketised non-personal relationship came into existence. In the system no longer there is assured employment or any employer on whom they can fall upon in times of distress. Further many of them have become unfit for hard work and today tribal labour is no longer in demand. Here again for this distress situation the migrants have played a decisive role. In the beginning, as migrants were in dire need of labour all efforts were made to woe them. In this they succeeded. Once they started mingling with the migrants the next strategy evolved was to extract hard work from the labour. They were offered liquor. Also as wage rate shot up the tribal labour got more and more addicted to liquor. This impacted on their health. Many tribal labourers have become incapacitated for normal work. Even today this form of exploitation is going on. Thus the tribes are recruited in-group for the seasonal work in the farm operated by the locals outside the state. For this labour especially the young and able bodied are recruited. The strategy was to extract hard work by offering liquor. By the time they return a good number of them are addicted to alcohol. Even denial of agreed wage is reported. Apart from this as some of them are women sexual abuse too is widespread. Another form of exploitation of the tribes is that they are used for most of the illegal activities of the migrants. These activities run on the lines of looting forest wealth mainly timber, ivory collection, hunting of wild animals for meat, felling of sandalwood trees etc. As the tribes are familiar with the interior of the forest for the movement and the transportation of the items they are deployed. All this is done at considerable risk to their life. A recent incident is worth mentioning. A group from the village accompanied by a tribal went to the Mysore forest for hunting and ivory collection. One of them was carrying a charged rifle and on the way when he accidentally fell another one got shooted on the thigh. He started crying loudly. This occurred very close to a forester's camp. Sensing the danger of being caught the injured was killed and buried by the side of a water pool. The diseased person left home in the guise of visiting a relative but came to be noticed as missing. In the meanwhile a wild animal unearthed the dead body. The news spread and the relatives identified this as the missing person. The gang was later arrested and they have confessed on the above lines.

The village is surrounded by thick forests on three sides. Attack of wild animals has become much more serious today. One of the reasons was the dwindling of the forest area. The problem is more serious with the tribal families who are settled on the fringe of the forests. Again while the well to do attempt to protect either by erecting compound wall or by drawing electrified wires on all sides it is the tribes who are becoming more vulnerable to the attack. Crop losses are heavy.

Problems have also a gender dimension. Specifically the developments have an adverse effect upon the employment opportunities of women, particularly tribal women. Paddy and other crops which are labour intensive and employ large number of women is disappearing and plantation crops have come to dominate the scene. In the existing pattern the one crop that provides some employment to women is ginger cultivation. Here again women are employed in weeding which is a subsidiary job. While employment and income loss is one side of the problem the other is the increasing role of females in sustaining the households. Tribal men have become lazy and addicted to alcohol. Thus there is less financial support for the households from the male members. In turn the women have come to shoulder the responsibilities for the sustenance of the households. The most distressing side effect of all this is that there is rising prostitution among the tribes.

The improved status and living conditions of the migrants too have its adverse influence on the tribes. Clearly there is demonstration effect. Thus to cope up with others the tribes spend extravagantly. We made a particular note of two specific cases. One of the tribal youth on leased in land planted banana and in the venture he was able to generate a surplus of about Rs. 1500. Instead of using it productively he brought a watch costing about the same amount and in his perception this was what in the society he should have.

In another instance a milch cattle was disposed off and with the money a cycle was bought. The argument was that many others have their own motorized transport and this is a basic minimum that he should have. Thus the improved standards of living of the migrants have a telling effect upon the tribes. In the daily life of all tribes including women the extravagance is most conspicuous. The tribes mainly patronise hotels and cinema theatres. To a certain extent it is also a fact that it is to cope up with other's style of living that many are induced to prostitution.

Apart from these direct forms of exploitation the migrants are misusing the protective law of the tribes. To state, tribal abuse has been made a serious offence in the state and is non-bailable if arrested on a complaint. The non-tribal migrants sometimes make the law to settle the personal disputes. A typical case may be mentioned. There was a boundary dispute between two neighbouring migrants. As pre-planned a tribal worker was deployed to fence the boundary by one of them and when the other disputed a false case was registered under the tribal abuse clause against him with the active support of the tribal worker. This forced the other to fall in line. Even some of the clever tribes are misusing the law to harass others on account of personal enmity.

To sum up it can be said that the migration has impacted upon the tribal population and their economy in various forms. There were beneficial as well as detrimental effects as far as the economy of the tribes are concerned. Introduction of new crops and cultivation practices were the beneficial ones. On this score however the benefits reaped by the tribes were marginal they being landless. Even if there was land the tribes are constrained to develop their farm. Being depended upon wage labour for sustenance they can hardly afford to stay away from work to develop their farm. Much needed finance too they lack for the land development. Accordingly we have found that proper land utilization leaves much to be desired in the case of tribes. One lone exception we came across. He was hard working and developed the land either by working at night or by staying away from outside work for some days. Of course his employer (he was permanently employed by a high caste Hindu) was very generous and extended help in developing the land. Another important quality was that he was uninfluenced by liquor and as a result of all this he was able to come out successfully compared to the other tribal households in the village we studied. On the whole while the benefit reaped out of agricultural development remained peripheral the benefit out of the diversification of the economy too by and large missed the tribes. Employment opportunities were on the rise. So also the wage rate. However as argued above the marketisation process has placed them in a disadvantageous position and hence here too the net benefit that accrued to them was questionable in nature. No doubt social and economic infrastructure developed. But here again as evidenced disproportionate benefit accrued to the migrants. Thus the beneficial effect of development on the tribal economy can be said as nominal. At the same time the detrimental effects can be found as large. Land alienation was the most important problem of all. Equally significant was the loss of access to common property resources. In fact this has deeply cut the source of livelihood of the tribes. The spread of alcoholism too has led to the erosion of the economic base of the tribes in a big way. On the whole it can therefore safely be concluded that migration has adversely impacted upon the economy of the tribes. No doubt the present day living conditions of the tribes are standing testimony to this. They are in an appalling condition. In consonance with this went their remark that they were much better off in the pre-migration period.

Chapter 8

Summary and Conclusions

Kerala is the most migratory state in India. There are several reasons to this. Some of them are quite unique also. On the social front in general and on the educational front in particular the level of performance of the state was exemplary. At the same time on the economic front the performance was quite dismal. This in turn led to serious unemployment problem and migration of people in search of employment outside the state as well as outside the country. Even historically the state has witnessed migration currents both internal and international. An internal movement, which sustained for considerable time period was the migration of people from Travancore to the northern region of Kerala called Malabar. In the beginning of this migration Travancore was a princely state and Malabar belonged to the Madras Presidency. The two regions stood apart on other accounts too. Malabar was then backward, thinly populated and there were vast underdeveloped areas. Travancore was somewhat developed and thickly populated. This migration began from the early decades of the 20th century around 1920's and continued for more than half a century. The migrants had peculiar features. Though in the beginning there were both large and small farmers by and large the sustained flow was confined to small cultivators with poor economic background. In the forefront were also the Christians. Though Christians dominated in the flow there was large number of non-Christians i.e. Hindus and Muslims. The migration was permanent. The main motivation was to make a reasonable living out of cultivation. Further they moved from a developed area to an underdeveloped area. As search was for cultivable land the settlement occurred in remote areas where cheap land was available. Further it also happened to be in the fringe of the forests, as there was vast scope for encroachment.

The migration had impacted upon the economic, social, political and cultural fronts of the region in a variety of ways. Also the migrants suffered a lot in the initial years of migration at the new settlements on several accounts. This was less heard outside. This study is an attempt to look into the impact of migration, the hardships faced by the migrants and to take stock of their accomplishments.

The study is with reference to the Pulpally village, which belongs to the Wayanad district of Malabar region. The village is situated in the interior of the district and is cut off from the main land route of the district. Forests surround the three sides of the village. Inspite of the locational disadvantages the development made by the village was unparalleled compared to any other settlements of the Travancore people in Malabar. There were also other reasons for the selection of the village for the study. It was one of the earliest human settlements as per the historical evidences. Even it is believed that the place had intimate connection with the

Ramayana epics. Apart from all this consequent upon migration the village witnessed several epoch making events on the social and political front. Hence this village was selected for the study. For detailed study a sample survey of 381 households were conducted. Out of them 194 were migrant households and the rest 187 were the native households. The natives comprised of 96 Chetty and 91 Tribal households.

At the time of migration the village was an uni-religious settlement of Hindus mainly comprised of Chetties and Tribals. There were several denominations of Chetties and Tribals. The Tribals were untouchable to the Chetties. Intra community though there was no untouchability there was segregation. This was much more among the Tribals. The pre-migration life of the people was one of primitive in which subsistence cultivation and food gathering provided the main source of livelihood. The Chetties were the cultivators and some of the Tribal sects like Paniyas were the agricultural labour. A feudalistic system also prevailed in the agricultural sector and in accordance to this the cultivators exercised masterly right over the workers. Even a slave system was then in existence in which the workers were contracted for one year by paying the slave money. Paddy was cultivated as a single crop in the wet land. In dry land other crops for home consumption was grown and it was shifting cultivation. Cattle ownership among the Chetty households was extensive and milk and milk products were abundant. However they were not maintained for commercial purpose. In the then prevailing situation as there was abundant land and labour cattle maintenance was virtually costless. Each tribal sect was engaged in their own avocation. Thus while some of them were agricultural labour, others were either cultivators, tool and pot makers. Still there were sects who were purely depended upon the forest products. While cultivation provided the main source of livelihood it was supplemented by food gathering by all the communities. While hunting provided the meat the streams flowing through out provided abundant fish. Market dependence was kept the minimum and the economy of the village can be characterised as more or less self-sufficient. To say, including tobacco they used to cultivate. Even on marriage occassions the market dependence was said as low. Cash transactions were very less and mostly barter system prevailed. Transport and communication facilities were conspicuous by its absence not to speak of trade and commerce. Medical facilities were absent. Housing was mostly of the hut type made of locally available materials mainly bamboo. Educational facilities badly lacked. Also they were very conservative too as all the communities held a common perception against much education. They brewed liquor for self-consumption. Chetty women were confined to household work. Though primitive and a low performing economy it was a self sufficient village economic system. A social structure was evolved for the sharing of each other's products. In the system each community had its own customary rights and responsibilities.

Though migration of Travancoreans to the Malabar region started from 1920's migration to Pulpally occurred much later. Some of the stray evidences indicated that first migrant came in 1948. As per our observation the migration continued up to 1984. The flow picked up from the middle of 1950's and the peak flow occurred during the 1965-71 period. In the history of this migration Pulpally migration became an important event. Most of the village lands at the time was in the possession of the Pulpally devaswom (temple). A part was made available for cultivation. Vast areas were uninhabited thick forest. Management of the temple was corrupt and inefficient. There was no demarcation of the land leased or sold. Therefore to state, the status of the land turned out to be that of common property. The result the land was encroaced on a massive scale by the migrants. While some of them purely encroached the land others in addition to the size of land deal made encroached the land. Only a few went by the size of the land deal made with the temple authorities. Thus among the sample households it was found that 52 migrant households resorted to pure encroachment over an area of 462.34 acres (8.89 acres per encroacher). Another 38 resorted to both purchase and encroachment and the size of encroachment on their part on an average came to 12.67 acres. Thus 90 encroachers on an average encroached 10.48 acres. Altogether among the sample migrants for every I acre land deal made it was found that 0.81 acre was encroached. Most of the encroachers belonged to the Christians followed by Muslims and Hindus. The land was very fertile too and this in fact gave added attraction for the migrants to grab Pulpally land. The migrants worked in close co-operation and unfailing unity in occupying the land and developing it. No doubt the temple authorities on their part attempted to evict them and hence guards were employed to remove or set fire to the huts, attach the work implements, destruction of crops etc. At the same time the migrants worked in close co-operation and got settled in the same land. When it became out of the control of the temple authorities a police camp was established and they too let loose eviction proceedings on the above lines. It thus became on the one side a law and order problem and on the other side a human right issue. The fight continued for some time. In this the Church came to support and assumed the leadership. The land also witnessed the rise of extreme revolutionary activities. Finally they were given protection under the Land Reforms Act. Thus ultimately ownership right was conferred no matter how the land came to be possessed.

Coming to the characteristics of the migrants a majority were Christians followed by Hindus and Muslims. Among the Hindus all the denominations are observable. This was the case with the Christians too as there were most of the rites in Pulpally. This was one of the unique features of Pulpally that a very diversified population in terms of religion/ caste is observable. By and large one of the common characteristics of the migrants was that most of them were from poor strata and their movement was in search of cultivable land. They were also young and most of them migrated with family. The migrants mainly originated from the Travancore region as nearly three fourth of them belonged to the Travancore region. They were fairly educated, as 94.51 percent were literate with some formal schooling. Migration was financed mainly by the disposal of their property at the native place. The initial years of their life in the place was known for hardships. Semi starvation, poor housing conditions, absence of social and economic infrastructures, non availability of goods, inhospitable climatic conditions, health problems and constant threat of wild animals to life and crops were the most important problems. In fact it was a life and death problem. The migrants also felt somewhat isolation in the beginning from the local communities due to certain misinformation. However much hostility they never faced from the local community. Soon the misgivings they were able to allay and they got absorbed in the host place.

Migration has brought about a total transformation of the village economy. The impact was also felt on the social, political and cultural spheres too. The village has become somewhat populated compared to other villages in the district. The most conspicuous development was the emergence of the Pulpally town. It has overtaken in terms of the growth of trade, transport, commerce etc. some of the old towns of the district. It has also emerged as one of the important trading centres for the agricultural products i.e hill products. This is inspite of the locational disadvantage of the village. Thus from a state of absence of a retail out let for essential goods the move was to a very mature trading and commerce centre. In terms of the development of roads, telecommunication, schools, hospitals, banking and other institutional development the village made an unparalleled development within a very short time. In all this the community participation and initiative was the other unique feature of Pulpally. In fact it is doubtful whether any other village in the whole of the Malabar region witnessed such an overall development. There does now exist a well-developed land and labour market. On the economic front the change was much more commendable. From subsistence farming the movement was to a most commercialised agriculture. Precisely the farmers have well responded to the profitable opportunities in agriculture. This is clearly manifest in the agricultural evolution in the village as over the period substantial changes in the cropping pattern took place. No doubt in the process the farmers were able to realise large economic prosperity. This in fact got reflected in the profound growth and diversification of the village economy. Still it is a fact that agriculture predominates. It can again be doubted in terms of land use and income generation whether there is any other village in the whole of the Malabar region.

Coming to an examination of the social and economic condition of the population of the village based on the sample survey we conducted it was found that there was on an average 5.44 persons per household with highest household size among the tribals and lowest among the Chetties. The sex ratio worked out to 930 females per 1000 males and it was highest among the tribal community and lowest among the Chetties. The proportion of young and teenaged population was high. At the same time the proportion of aged population was low. Category wise the proportion of young population was high among the native chetties and tribes and at the same time the proportion of old aged was low among the two communities. Marital status of females stood better than males and the status was better as far as the tribals are concerned. Majority were nuclear families as in the total 43.04 percent were only joint families. Joint families were highest 49.48 percent among the migrants. Going by the educational level of the population and current educational enrolment rate of children it was found that the population has come a long way on the road of educational development. Among all, the migrant population was relatively better-placed in educational development and the tribals were very backward. Still importantly we noted that they have become more receptive to education and the age-old conservatism has gone among all the communities.

On an average there was 2.36 workers per household and work participation rate comes to 43.41

percent. Child labour was observed as very low even among the tribals communities. At the same time the work participation rate of the aged above 61 was found as significantly on the higher side particularly among the male. Work participation rate was highest among the tribals followed by the chetties. The lowest was among the migrants. This was true of all age groups and sex. Quite revealingly it was noticed that the female participation in work was high among the chetties relative to the migrants while it was the other way in the initial years of migration. This was the result of status improvement on the part of the migrant households. At the same time many Chetty households witnessed deterioration in the status. Occupational structure revealed that agriculture still continue to absorb more than four fifth of the workers. Still some employment diversification resulted and the diversification was also found as more among the migrant households. The economic status of the households were examined in terms of the assets ownership including current land ownership, housing conditions, ownership of consumer durable goods and per capita expenditure. Looked from these angles it was revealed that a number of households had reasonable living conditions. In particular the economic status of the migrant community was found as better than others. The condition of the tribal households was found as one of appalling in terms of housing and living conditions. They were also poorly endowed with all types of assets. To state a significant number of them were landless.

Here what is significant to note is that several of the villages in Malabar witnessed migration. But the developmental impact felt by the Pulpally village was not felt by any of them. On this we are to state that the migrant people in particular the Christians were very enterprising, had vision and a plan. They were endowed with leadership qualities and worked in unity. What is significant to note is that though people came from various places they worked in unity. Perhaps the eviction problem they faced in the settlement enabled them to unite and fight. In the process several developed the leadership quality. Whatever the case we are to say that the collective action of the people of Pupally had gone a long way in developing the village. As a blessing in disguise came the attack of the Naxals as this too played a significant role in giving a boost to the developmental activities particularly transport and communication.

The developmental impact of migration was found as commendable on the village economy and its people. But at the same time distressingly there were negative impacts too. Disparity in development was one. While some of the areas mainly concentrated by the migrant community has become more developed other areas have witnessed only peripheral development. To state there are areas as backward as before. While this is one dimension of disparity the other is the disparity between various communities. In general while the migrants have become prosperous the spillover of benefits to the natives were only marginal. Within the migrants it was the Christian community who effected the best status improvement. Among the natives while Chetty households have been able to effect some improvement the tribals have been found as adversely affected. In fact the overall conclusion that we have been able to draw is that the condition of tribals had worsened. The growing economy of the village generated new opportunities. Most of them were made use of by the migrants in general and the Christian migrants in particular. Here the participation of the natives was practically insignificant. At the same time there were forces at work in eroding considerably the economic base of the tribal population. Land alienation was one. The other was the liquor addiction. Thus a situation has emerged that they now purely depend on wage labour. Though developments in the labour market front led to a spillover of benefits in the form of rising wage they have become vulnerable to the markets for commodities being depended upon the market. Thus on the whole the development process has led to a sharp economic divide between areas and classes. Another important side effect of migration is that the eco system has come to confront pressure. There was vast destruction of forests and associated with this while on the one hand there was loss of animal and plant life on the other hand they cut deep into the traditional livelihood of the tribal population. Vast areas, which were thick forest with rich flora and fauna has been transformed into land for human settlements with intensive agricultural production. Intensive agricultural practices also led to the degradation of the soil. Some of the agricultural practices too like tilling are causing soil erosion. Ground water is also over exploited and water table is fastly on the decline. Even the topography of the village has undergone change. On the whole the study comes to the conclusion that considerable environmental cost has been incurred on account of this migration. What is more distressing to note is that even now this is taking place at a very significant scale and some of the instances illustrated here are well indicative of this.

The agricultural economy of the village is also facing crisis. Rising cost, falling agricultural productivity and product prices all are pausing fresh challenges to the farmers.

On the social front too there were several impacts. The problem of unwed mothers, widespread alcoholism, deployment of tribals for certain illegal activities of the migrants were some of them.

In the light of the above findings we make the following recommendations.

The first and foremost need of the hour is to put an end to the indiscriminate destruction of the forestland and the looting of the forest wealth which even now continues at an alarming scale. The attitude of the government in arresting the issue appears as one of soft. The administration is also playing second fiddle to the encroachers. What is needed is strict enforcement of the existing laws. In case of violation harsh punishment need to be given to act as a deterrent. Side by side the government has also to harden its attitude towards the organized lobby of settlers. Under no circumstance recourse to legislative action be adopted to protect the encroachers.

Natural resource management is becoming more and more inefficient in these hill tracts. This is especially the case with the soil and water. What requires is popularisation of crops best suited to the soil and agro-climatic conditions of the hill tracts. The agricultural department have to evolve area specific crop pattern. So also the ideal farm practices have to be evolved. This needs to be popularised by way of training programme for the farmers and other extension works. Further the official assistance for crops other than the one suitable for the area may be withdrawn. Side by side those adopting the non ideal crops may be penalised. Incentive schemes may be evolved and made avaliable for the adoption of ideal crops and their practices. Further in the conservation of water and its most economical use much needed effort is called for on the part of the authorities. Ground water needs to be conserved and its exploitation restrained by suitable regulations. Training programmes can go a long way in popularizing the water conservation techniques.

There is widespread over exploitation of the land resources in the village by intensive agricultural operation on dry land. This is not an environmentally sound practice and in the long run how far this is sustainable is open to doubt. For short-term gains the long run interest is compromised. An optimum level of land use needs to be encouraged by policy intervention at the official level. Say official assistance may be withdrawn in the case of a much intensive land use.

Paddy fields are kept fallow. So also there is large-scale conversion of paddy fields for other crops mainly plantation crops. This should be discouraged in the interest of promoting some amount of food self-sufficiency at the village level as well as food security. Conversion of paddy lands for plantation crops may be strictly prohibited. Even if permitted a penal lump sum amount may be collected depending upon the size of land and the collected amount may be ear marked for the promotion of paddy cultivation.

Indiscriminate way by which the chemical fertilizers are promoted too needs to be restrained. Bio-fertilizers needs to be encouraged and in villages like Pulpally there is vast scope for this. The agriculture department has to take an initiative in imparting the much needed awareness programme.

To protect the tribals a number of welfare measures have been evolved and protective legislation brought forth. Also in the name of development programmes sizable resources have been channeled. However inspite of all this the conditions of the tribal population has not shown any perceptible change. Most tragically in their perception their condition has worsoned compared to the earlier period. Here our view is that a multifaceted approach may be adopted for their time bound development. On these lines goes some of the following suggestions.

A desire for self- improvement needs to be inculcated among them. This is now utterly lacking. For each unit of tribal household say 50 houses a voluntary social activist from among them may be selected and the needed training and education may be imparted to him. He may have to be trained in such a way as to act as a catalyst for change. What is required is an awakening among them.

We have found that hardly any employment benefit out of the reservation policy has come to be enjoyed by this section. The policy needs to be stream-lined in such a way as to make available opportunities to each category more or less equitably. Employment provision at least for one generation is a better way to uplift them compared to any other schemes.

The tribal land alienation is an age- old problem. Though legislative and other measures were adopted materially no progress has been made on this front. Thus the tribals have become more deprived in the post migration period. The issue is riddled with problems. On the one side the formulae evolved by the government is not acceptable to the Tribals. On the other side the demand of the tribals are at loggerheads with what is articulated by the settlers. Both of them are organized and agitating. There are also implementation problems. No surprise the government is in a dilemma. It is high time for the government to act. On this our view is that all the tribal land held in excess of one acre may be taken away and restored to the tribals. What is required is a political consensus and a commitment on the part of the government. This is also one of the method to decolonise the tribals as colonised life can be observed as one of the reason for their current plight.

Left to themselves the tribals are less able to develop and exploit the land resources. Here the prospects of co- operative organization for the development of the tribal land may be thought of with the effective coordination of the agricultural department.

Our field observation has revealed that there is substantial socio economic change among the families of tribals with inter- religious/ inter- caste marriage. In fact in the course of the fieldwork we observed that the most educated were the children of these families (some of them were studying for higher secondary course). The living conditions and the economic status have made notable change among them compared to the rest. Though on an extensive scale the scope for the popularization of the practice is strictly limited it needs to be encouraged for which special incentives may be made available. Incentives may be administered for the couple and their offspring. It can go on the lines of preferential allotment of land and house, assets endowment under the poverty eradication programme and even specific quota of job reservation out of the tribal quota to their children limited to one generation.

The social problem of unwed mothers needs to be addressed. What is needed is a permanent solution. It can be argued that there are pitfalls in the official approach to the problem by way of the organization of rehabilitation programme and legal redressal. As we have been able to learn the rehabilitation schemes have come to act as an added incentive to indulge in such practice in the prevailing situation. Such an apprehension is widely there in the minds of the people. We also feel that there is some grain of truth in this. In view of this such provision has to be restricted to the victims already reported and fresh cases should not be entertained. In no uncertain words this should be communicated to the concerned society. Also as most of the sexual relation occurred voluntarily the very legal action in a penal way intiated against the male appears to be somewhat discriminatory. In view of this in order to give a deterrent effect the female should also be tried and made at least lightly punishable unless she is induced to have sex forcibly.

In addressing to the problems of the communities in general there is official apathy at the implementation level. Thus the magnitude of the benefit that trickle downs to the tribals are only a fraction. The most telling feature of this is non- issue of ration cards. A number of families we surveyed did not have the ration card and this was inspite of the best efforts they made to get it. The administration has to be made tribal friendly.

Among the tribals now a days there is a widespread belief that it is the responsibility of the state to maintain them with the effect they are becoming lazy and demanding. Even for petty things official machinery is approached. For e.g. it has been pointed out to us that for replacement of one or two roof tiles they approach the officials even if it meant abstaining from one- day work. Such a situation has arisen, as there are a number of schemes including petty provisions. Instead of variety of programmes it is effective to have few programmes say employment generation schemes, education and housing so that the resources can be concentrated on them. Even in the case of housing provision when once the house is made available its maintenance should be their responsibility.

Many tribals are less aware of what all entitlements are there for them. This can be attributed as one of the reasons for corruption, which is prevalent in the system of administration. What is required is giving wide publicity to the tribal welfare schemes. An awareness campaign may be organized at the grass root level and once they are aware of them they can claim their rightful share. If a social worker as suggested above is deployed he can contribute much in this sphere.

The problem of alchoholism among the tribals needs to be tackled on a war footing. Liquor (arrack) is illicitly transported from the neighboring state. This may be prevented by making effective the existing control mechanism. Side by side the people may be enlightened about the ill effects by constant persuasion and organizing anti liquor campaigns.

Even tribal law is misused, on the one side by the outside elements and on the other side by the tribals. It is desirable that a village level committee with representation to several interest groups and prominent social activists be constituted. They may be consulted at the stage of investigation for initiating legal course of action. This can go a long way in checking the misuse.

So also those attempting to misuse the law should be subjected to punishment.

In the course of our investigation a very paradoxical situation we came across in respect of the policy of reservation. There were several Hindu communities other than scheduled castes who are socially and economically backward. Say for e.g. Kalanadies, Kunduvadians and some of the other categories of Chetties. While some category of Chetties are made eligible for reservation under the category of Other Backward Communities this is denied to other denominations. An identical treatment may be given to all of them, as their status is more or less identical.

Last but not least as far as possible the people must be able to settle down in their own native land by which considerable social and economical hardships can be avoided. This calls for opening up economic opportunities in places of human concentration. Though this migration has led to growth an unrestrained movement has led to several social and economic problems including environmental degradation and deprivation to the marginalised sections. It is in view of this that we suggest the need for the restriction of this type of movement.

Index

Christian Households, 94, 104

E

G

H